Speechcraft

Speechcraft

Workbook for International TA Discourse

Laura D. Hahn

Wayne B. Dickerson

MICHIGAN SERIES IN ENGLISH FOR
ACADEMIC & PROFESSIONAL PURPOSES

Ann Arbor

THE UNIVERSITY OF MICHIGAN PRESS

PREFACE

Speechcraft: Workbook for International TA Discourse accompanies its core text, *Speechcraft: Discourse Pronunciation for Advanced Learners.* This workbook focuses on the language that international teaching assistants (ITAs) in U.S. universities need in order to communicate effectively in the classroom, lab, and office hours settings.

The *Speechcraft* materials consist of a core textbook, workbooks for specific audiences that expand on and contextualize the content of the core textbook, and accompanying audiotapes. Details about the focus and organization of the *Speechcraft* materials can be found in the Preface of the core text.

The textbook and workbooks interrelate as follows.

Speechcraft

	Introductory Topics	
Textbook	**Groundwork**	
	Academic/Professional Terms	Workbooks
	Discourse Level Topics	
Textbook	Discourse Foundations	
	Discourse Domains	Workbooks
	Word Level Topics	
Textbook	Word Foundations	
Textbook (Patterns)	Word Stress Domains	Workbooks (Practice and Review)
	Construction Stress	Workbooks
	Supplementary Topics	
Textbook	Suggestions for Instructors	
Textbook	Vowel and Consonant Prediction Patterns	
(for units in Textbook)	Answers	(for units in Workbooks)
	Oral Practice Projects	Workbooks
	Checklist for Covert Rehearsal	Workbooks

The materials in this workbook are also useful in preparing for the SPEAK or TSE exams; additional suggestions and practice can be found in *Toward Speaking Excellence: The Michigan Guide to Maximizing Your Performance on the TSE® and SPEAK® Tests* by Dean Papajohn (Ann Arbor: University of Michigan Press, 1998).

CONTENTS

Academic Terms

General Academic Terms

One of the requirements for success as an international TA is that you be able to pronounce words in the vocabulary of academic English. In order to increase your intelligibility when you speak in English about your field of study, you need to take responsibility for pronouncing important words correctly. *Speechcraft* will be able to help you analyze many of those words.

Choose forty words from the "General Academic Terms" list that follows. Make choices based on frequency of occurrence and difficulty of pronunciation. You will practice these words throughout the course and will be responsible for them.

Write the words here.

_____	_____	_____	_____
_____	_____	_____	_____
_____	_____	_____	_____
_____	_____	_____	_____
_____	_____	_____	_____
_____	_____	_____	_____
_____	_____	_____	_____
_____	_____	_____	_____
_____	_____	_____	_____
_____	_____	_____	_____

abbreviation
absence
academic
acceleration
account
accumulate
accuracy
adequate
administration
adversity
alleviate
allocate
allowance
analysis
analyze
anomalous
anomaly
anonymous
antecedent
apparent
appendix
apply
appropriate
approximation
ascertain
assimilation
assume
assumption
asymmetrical
atypical
augment
authentic
authenticity
axiom
axiomatic

behaviorist
bias

calculus
category

cause
challenge
character
characteristic
chronological
classify
cognitive
colleague
communicative
comparative
compel
competency
comprehensive
computer
concept
condition
confidence
congruent
consensus
conservative
consultant
continuum
contradictory
corollary
correct
criteria
critical
critique
crucial

data
decrease
deduce
define
definition
definitive
denote
description
design
deteriorate
diagnosis

dichotomy
differ
difference
different
differentiate
discipline
disclosure
discovery
discriminatory
dissertation
dominant
dynamic

effect
efficacy
elicit
eliminate
empirical
employee
equal
event
exclusive
exemplify
experiment
experimental
expertise
explanatory
exponential
extend
external

fallacy
fallible
familiarize
feedback
format
formula
frequency
frequent
fundamental

generate

gradual

graph

history

homogeneity

horizontal

humanities

hypothesis

illustrate

implication

include

inclusive

increase

induction

industrialize

information

informative

initial

innovative

instructional

instrumental

interrupt

introductory

invent

irrelevant

judge

kilometer

knowledge

lecture

liberal

literal

literature

magnitude

marginal

maximum

mean

measure

median

mediator

metaphor

minimum

model

mystery

normal

objective

obligatory

obvious

occasional

occur

opinion

optimum

original

parallel

pedagogical

permutation

perspective

phenomenon

picturesque

plagiarism

polemics

portion

position

possible

practitioner

precautionary

precede

predominant

preliminary

previous

primary

principle

probability

problem

procedure

proportion

prototype

qualify

qualitative

quantify

quantitative

quarter

quartile

question

range

rapid

rare

rate

rationale

rationalize

reaction

reduce

redundancy

refer

reference

relationship

relative

relevant

replacement

representative

requirement

research

reserve

respectively

response

return

rigorous

secondary

signature

similar

similarity

simultaneous

situation

solution

specialize

specific

specify

stimulus

study

subsequent

substantial

sufficient

summary

supposition

syllabus

synopsis

synthesis

synthetic

system

technical

technique

technology

textbook

theorem

theoretical

theory

tolerance

traditional

transfer

trivialize

typical

unique

university

value

variable

variation

verify

vertical

volunteer

zero

SPECIFIC ACADEMIC TERMS

One of the requirements for success as an ITA is that you be able to pronounce words in your field of study. In order to increase your intelligibility when you speak in English about your field of study, you need to take responsibility for pronouncing important words correctly. *Speechcraft* will be able to help you analyze many of those words.

Choose forty words from your own academic discipline. Make choices based on frequency of occurrence and difficulty of pronunciation. You will practice these words throughout the semester and will be responsible for them.

Write the words here.

_____	_____	_____	_____
_____	_____	_____	_____
_____	_____	_____	_____
_____	_____	_____	_____
_____	_____	_____	_____
_____	_____	_____	_____
_____	_____	_____	_____
_____	_____	_____	_____
_____	_____	_____	_____
_____	_____	_____	_____

DISCOURSE DOMAINS

Discourse Domains expand on the information in Discourse Foundations in *Speechcraft*'s core text. Discourse Domains cover specific types of language that international TAs need in the classroom and lab and during office hours. The topics may be studied in any order, according to students' needs.

D-8

COMPARING AND CONTRASTING

☛ EXERCISE 1.   a. Listen to the following passage.
                            b. Mark the primary stress with ● according to what you hear. There may be more than one primary stress in some message units.

Before we begin teaching, | many of us have either a positive attitude | or a negative attitude | toward American students. This comes in part from a tendency to think that all students are alike. But they're not all alike. That's why it's so challenging to understand them.

For example, | some students are abstract thinkers, | and some are concrete thinkers. Some have liberal values, | and some have conservative values. Some students find the sciences easier than the languages, | or rhetoric easier than physics. And for some, | socializing is more important than studying—and the reverse is true for others.

It is also helpful to think about yourself. | Are you an energetic person | or a relaxed person? Do you have high standards | or low standards? We often expect our students to approach things in the same way, | but that doesn't always happen. And unfortunately, | we often favor the students we identify with | and disfavor those we misunderstand.

Understanding our students isn't the easiest task in the world, | but it's one of the most rewarding. We can appreciate differences | but still treat all students fairly and equally.

The Structures of Contrasts

There are six different kinds of contrasts that can be made, classified as follows.

1. choice questions
2. *either . . . or*
3. [*x*, not *y*] and [not *x*, but *y*]
4. contradictions
5. contrasts in parallel phrases
6. Noun (comparative) than Noun

Contrasts are most often words. Sometimes, however, parts of words—even single syllables—are in contrast.

This lesson focuses on two-way contrasts. The next lesson (Lists and Series) includes contrasts that have more than two elements.

The Sounds of Contrasts

Primary Stress. In each type of contrast, primary stress goes on the word(s)—or syllable(s)—carrying the contrasted information. The contrasts may be made across message units or within message units. In some cases, there may be more than one primary stress in a message unit.

If the primary stress is not on the last word, remember to make all syllables after the primary stress on a low, even pitch and with a quicker voice, so that the primary stress stands out clearly from the surrounding syllables.

Intonation. The nonfinal message units have the rise-to-mid-range melody. The final message unit has the low-range melody. Remember that you can use the pitch jump and pitch drop versions in any combination.

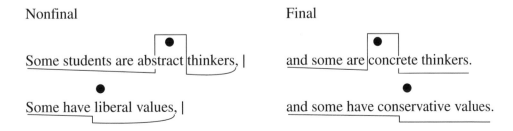

Nonfinal

Some students are abstract thinkers, |

Some have liberal values, |

Final

and some are concrete thinkers.

and some have conservative values.

Contrast Type 1. Choice questions

This contrast type is discussed in detail in Discourse Domains D-10: Choice Questions and Answers.

Are you an energetic person | or a relaxed person?

Do you have high standards | or low standards?

Contrast Type 2. *Either . . . or*

In this case, the elements in focus represent the choices. *Whether . . . or* statements also work the same way.

Many of us have either a positive attitude | or a negative attitude | toward Americans.

Notice that the contrast can also come in a syllable of a word.

Tell whether each argument represents inductive reasoning | or deductive reasoning.

☞ **EXERCISE 2.**   Dialogs and Passages
a. Mark the primary stress with ●.
b. Read each dialog or passage aloud.

Example:

For your final project, | you can either design an experiment | or critique an experiment.

Dialog 1. Two students talking

   A: I see you're reading *Don Quixote*.

   B: Yes. We can read either the English version | or the Spanish version.

Dialog 2. In a statistics class

   A: I don't know how to tell | whether to risk a type 1 error | or a type 2 error.

   B: It depends on the purpose of the experiment.

Passage 1. In a religious studies class

       Let's classify the following religions | by telling whether they are poly-theistic | or monotheistic.

Passage 2. A student discussing his workload

       I have more homework than I expected. I'm going to either audit this class | or drop it.

☛ **EXERCISE 3.**   Incomplete Dialogs
             a. Complete the following dialogs with a partner.
             b. Mark the primary stress with ●.
             c. Read each dialog aloud with your partner.

Dialog 1

   A: How do the students here get to campus?

   B: Most of them either _____ to school | or _____ to school.

Dialog 2

   A: What are you doing after class?

   B: I'm so busy. I can't decide whether to _____ first | or to _____ first.

> ## Contrast Type 3. [*x*, not *y*] and [not *x*, but *y*]

These constructions have three main components. The *x* and *y* represent the two elements being contrasted—and each receives primary stress. The **negative** word then signals what the contrast is, although it does not receive primary stress.

        ●   ●

You'll need to evaluate the facts, | not just memorize them.
           (*x*)   (not)   (*y*)

                          ●

Understanding our students isn't the easiest task in the world, | but it's one of the
                         (not)   (*x*)   (but)

      ●

most rewarding.
  (y)

☞ **EXERCISE 4.**   Dialogs and Passages
                    a. Mark the primary stress with ●.
                    b. Read each dialog or passage aloud.

Example:

                    ●   ●

I'm going to take physics this semester | and not wait until next semester.

Dialog 1. Two students talking

A: We should have started our homework before we went to that party.

B: Well, | that was your idea, | not mine.

Dialog 2. In an ESL class

A: Why is it so difficult to learn English?

B: It must be because of the pronunciation.

A: OK. Pronunciation may be one of the reasons, | but it's not the only reason.

Passage 1. A student talking about another student's grade

> I can't believe he got a C. I admit, | it wasn't an A paper, | but maybe it was a B paper.

Passage 2. In a biology class

> Look at this cell again—it has a true nucleus. So it must be a eukaryote, | not a prokaryote.

☛ **EXERCISE 5.**   Incomplete Sentences
       a. Complete the following sentences with a partner.
       b. Mark the primary stress with ●.
       c. Take turns reading each sentence aloud.

Contrast adjectives

      _____'s a _____ class, not a _____ class.
     (name of class)   (*x*)   (*y*)

Contrast verbs

     I never _____ before this class, but I _____ before this class.
            (*x*)   (*y*)

Contrast nouns

     I had Professor _____ for my _____ class, not Professor
                  (*x*)   (name of class)

     _____.
       (*y*)

Contrast Type 4. Contradictions

In this type of contrast, the first utterance makes a proposition, and the second utterance directly contradicts it.

                                                     ●

This comes in part from a tendency to think that all students are alike.

             ●

But they're not all alike.

Contradictions are more common in conversation, where speaker B's reaction is a contradiction to something speaker A said. Speaker B highlights the contrast by stressing one of the following.

- "not" or a negative contraction. If the verb being contradicted is positive, use "not" or a contraction to contradict the verb. The "not" or negative contraction receives primary stress.

    Example 1:

                       ●   ●

    A: Since you're a senior, | I thought you'd have already taken rhetoric.

                  ●   ●

    B: But I'm not a senior. I'm a sophomore.

    Example 2:

                                                         ●

    A: What did your TA say when you handed in your assignment late?

             ●   ●

    B: I didn't hand it in. I'm still working on it.

- The auxiliary verb. If the verb to be contradicted is negative, then use a form of the verb *be* or *do* if there is no other auxiliary. This form receives primary stress.

Example 1:

A: It doesn't seem like you're enjoying our class. Is everything OK?

B: I am enjoying it. I've just been really sick.

Example 2:

A: I was hoping you'd join our *aerobics class. (Implication: "You didn't join.")

B: I did join. But so far I've been too busy to go.

- The element containing the "correction" to speaker A's utterance

    Example 1:

    A: So according to the *Doppler effect, | the observer in front of the

    truck hears the lower frequency, | right?

    B: I don't think so. I think he hears the higher frequency.

    Example 2:

    A: I have a lot of reading to do for biology. This week we're talking

    about DNA, | and I don't even understand it.

    B: You're really behind! We're already on RNA.

---

*compound noun

☞ **EXERCISE 6.**   Dialogs
a. Mark the primary stress with ●.
b. Read each dialog aloud.

Example:

                     ●   ●

A: I can't finish this dissertation! It's impossible!

              ●   ●

B: But you can finish. Just take it one day at a time.

Dialog 1. A student (A) asks the history TA (B) a question.

A: Why did Britain support Germany in World War I?

B: Actually, they didn't support Germany. They supported France and Russia.

Dialog 2. Two music students talking

A: Are you going to the recital?

B: Of course—I'm performing in the recital! I'm accompanying the soloist.

Dialog 3. Two graduate students talking

A: Why didn't you apply for an assistantship?

B: I did apply. But I applied too late, | and everything was already taken.

☞ **EXERCISE 7.**   Incomplete Dialogs
a. Complete the following dialogs with a partner.
b. Mark the primary stress with ●.
c. Read each dialog aloud with your partner.

Dialog 1

A: Why don't you like _____?

B: But I do like _____. I just never told you.

Dialog 2

    A: You're from _____ (country), | right?

    B: Actually, I'm not from _____. I'm from _____.

Dialog 3

    A: You like _____ music, | don't you?

    B: Actually, I like _____ music.

Contrast Type 5. Contrasts in parallel phrases

In this case, there are two (or more) facets to the contrast. When both facets of the comparison are in the same message unit, there are two primary stresses in each message unit.

      ●   ●   ●

We often favor the students we identify with | and disfavor those we don't

      ●

understand.

Here, "favor" contrasts with "disfavor," and "identify with" contrasts with "don't understand." And the two message units are parallel in structure.

The facets of the contrast can also be in separate message units.

      ●   ●   ●   ●

If it's below 32 degrees, | it's a solid; if it's above 32 degrees, | it's a liquid.

☛ **EXERCISE 8.**   Passages
                         a. Mark the primary stress with ●.
                         b. Read each passage aloud.

Example:

      ●   ●   ●   ●

In some cultures, | copying is a form of praise. But in others, | it's a form of deceit.

Passage 1

The numerator goes on the top, | and the denominator goes on the bottom.

Passage 2

On the first test, | you'll be asked to describe a *balance sheet; | on the second test, | you'll be asked to use a balance sheet.

Passage 3

Put your references in alphabetical order | and your figures in numerical order.

Passage 4

Justin prefers learning by the inductive method, | but Bill prefers the deductive method.

☞ **EXERCISE 9.**   Your Own Parallel Contrasts
    a. Choose one of the pairs of words and write a parallel contrast sentence. You will have to supply another facet for the contrast.
    b. Mark the primary stresses with ●.
    c. Take turns reading each sentence aloud with a partner.

first semester/second semester	optimist/pessimist
right hand/left hand	work/relax
open-book exam/closed-book exam	speak/understand (languages)
first choice/second choice	use a pencil/use a pen
realist/idealist	like/dislike

          ●   ●   ●   ●
Example: I write with my left hand, | and I eat with my right hand.

---

*compound noun

> ### Contrast Type 6. Noun (comparative) than Noun

In these types of contrasts, one noun phrase is compared with another using the comparative form of an adjective. A comparative form can be either [Adjective + -er ("easier") + "than"] or ["more" + Adjective + "than"]. In these cases, the part of each noun phrase that is being compared receives primary stress.

                          ●   ●

Some students find the sciences easier than the languages.

             ●   ●

For some, | socializing is more important than studying.

      ●   ●

The southern climate is more humid than the northern climate.

        ●   ●

Playing a fair game is more important than playing a good game.

☛ **EXERCISE 10.**   Passages
                            a. Mark each primary stress with ●.
                            b. Read each passage aloud.
                            c. Then tell whether you agree or disagree with the statement. Explain your answer.

1. *Graduate students are more serious than *undergraduate students.

2. Professors make better instructors than *teaching assistants.

3. American food is healthier than Japanese food.

4. Cooperation is better than competition.

5. Big universities are more prestigious than small universities.

6. Lecturing is harder than leading discussions.

7. Speaking in English is more difficult than writing in English.

8. Speaking in English is more difficult than speaking in Chinese.

9. Going to a party is more fun than going to a concert.

10. Going to a party is more fun than hosting a party.

---

*compound noun

☞ **EXERCISE 11.**   In Your Own Field of Study
For each of the six types of contrast,
  a. Write a dialog or short passage that you would use in
     your own academic field.
  b. Mark each primary stress with ●.
  c. Read each dialog or passage aloud.

Example 1:   Choice questions
In a literature class

                     ●   ●

A: Is this poem a sonnet | or an ode?

             ●

B: It's an ode.

Example 2:   *Either . . . or*
In a philosophy class

                 ●

A: What kind of reasoning was this?

                   ●   ●

B: I think it was either a literal analogy | or a figurative analogy.

        ●   ●

A: Right. Which was it?

            ●   ●

C: It was a figurative analogy, | because the two things were essentially dif-
      ferent.

Example 3:   [*x,* not *y*] and [not *y,* but *x*]
In an educational psychology class

                                       ●

Someone give me an example of a test which has a lot of construct validity |

            ●

but not a lot of face validity.

Example 4:   Contradictions
In a geology class

●

A: Doesn't the temperature inside the earth decrease with depth?

●   ●

B: Actually, it increases. At first, | it increases at a rate of 48 degrees Celsius

●

per mile.

Example 5:   Parallel phrases
In a physiology class

●   ●   ●   ●

Plot the *heart rate on the *y* axis | and the *contraction size on the *x* axis.

Example 6:   Noun (comparative) than Noun
In a geography class

●   ●   ●   ●

In terms of area, | Indonesia is larger than Japan. But in terms of population, |

●   ●

Japan is larger than Indonesia.

---

*compound noun

D-9

LISTS AND SERIES

☞ **EXERCISE 1.** Listen to the following passage twice.
a. The first time, mark the message units with a bar symbol (|) according to what you hear.
b. The second time, mark the primary stress in each message unit with ● according to what you hear.

Welcome to English 115. Let me tell you a little bit about our class. We meet at 4:00 P.M. on Mondays, Wednesdays, and Fridays. The topic is poetry: we're going to be reading it, analyzing it, and even writing it. I expect you to come to class every day, because participation will be a part of your grade.

In terms of supplies, you'll need a notebook, an audiocassette tape, a floppy disk, and access to a computer. There is also a textbook, *An Anthology of Twentieth-Century Poetry*. It's available at the University Bookstore, Follett's, and the library.

In this class you'll be taking three exams, writing five short papers, doing a take-home final, and participating in one group project. I know it sounds like a lot, but it's going to be manageable. Do you have any questions so far?

In lists and series, primary stress and pitch move go on the last content word in the new information or on the last function word if there is no new content word.

A rise-to-mid-range melody is used for each member of the list except the last in a sentence, which has a low-range melody.

The Structure of Lists and Series

Lists and series are common in speech. They are made up of three or more words or phrases in a row. They are more or less parallel in construction.

We meet at 4:00 P.M. on *Mondays, Wednesdays, and Fridays.*
In this class you'll be *taking three exams, writing five short papers, doing a take-home final, and participating in one group project.*

The Sound of Lists and Series

Message Units. Each member in the list or series is a separate message unit.

We meet at 4:00 P.M. on Mondays, | Wednesdays, | and Fridays.
In this class you'll be taking three exams, | writing five short papers, | doing a take-home final, | and participating in one group project.

Primary Stress. Each message unit has its own primary stress. Primary stress goes on the last content word in the new information or on the last function word if there is no new content word.

Intonation. There is some variability in the intonation of lists and series. However, it will be clear that you are signaling a list if you follow these guidelines.

- Except for the last member, each member of the list uses a rise-to-mid-range melody.
- The last member has a low-range melody if it is the last phrase in the sentence.

Remember that you can use the pitch jump version or the pitch drop version for each melody pattern.

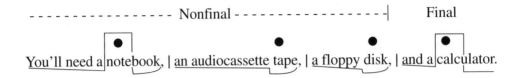

☛ **EXERCISE 2.**   Lists and Series in Classroom Talk
a. Mark the message units with a bar symbol (|).
b. Mark the primary stress in each message unit with ●.
c. Read each sentence aloud with a partner.

1. In order to get started, you need to boot up the computer, put in a diskette, and open an application.

2. For this set of numbers, find the mean, the standard variance, and the standard deviation.

3. The characters in this novel were young, innocent, and in love.

4. For Brazil, Ecuador, Peru, and Chile, write down the capital, the population, the *monetary unit, and the major exports.

5. Wherever you are, whatever you do, whenever you can, try to think in English.

6. You'll need to do observations in the lab, on campus, and in the community.

7. When you're finished with the test, put down your pencil, turn your paper over, and raise your hand.

8. I'll be in my office after the *discussion section, after the lecture, and before 10:00 A.M.

9. The first time you do a *Gram stain, be sure to do it slowly, carefully, and steadily.

10. For your group presentation, be sure to decide who'll talk first, second, third, and fourth.

---

*compound noun

☞ **EXERCISE 3.** Lists and Series in Quotations
a. Mark the message units with a bar symbol (|).
b. Mark the primary stress in each message unit with ●.
c. Read each quotation aloud with a partner.

Eat, drink, and be merry.

I came, I saw, I conquered.

—Julius Caesar

Early to bed and early to rise makes a man healthy, wealthy, and wise.

—Benjamin Franklin

Colors fade, temples crumble, empires fall, but wise words endure.

—Edward Thorndike

I hear and I forget; I see and I remember; I do and I understand.

—Chinese proverb

I desire to see the time when education, and by its means, morality, sobriety, enterprise,
and industry, shall become much more general than at present.

—Abraham Lincoln

Our knowledge is the amassed thought and experience of innumerable minds: our language, our science, our religion, our opinions, our fancies.

—Ralph Waldo Emerson

For without words, in friendship, all thoughts, all desires, all expectations are born and
shared, with joy that is unacclaimed.

—Kahlil Gibran

Contrasts in Parallel Phrases

Because lists are parallel in construction, sometimes each message unit repeats
one or more of the same words. In these cases, the repeated words are not in focus—instead the focus is on the word or words that are different in each member
in the series. In such cases we place primary stress on the last word in the new or
different information in each message unit.

In this example, "poetry" is not in focus, since it is repeated in each message unit. Therefore it will not receive primary stress even though it appears to be the last new content word in the first message unit.

                    ●   ●   ●

We're going to be reading poetry, | analyzing poetry, | and even writing poetry.

   ●   ●   ●

Hear no evil, | see no evil, | speak no evil.

☞ **EXERCISE 4.**   Lists and Series in Parallel Phrases
            a. Mark the message units with a bar symbol (|).
            b. Mark the primary stress in each message unit with ●.
            c. Read each sentence aloud with a partner.

1. Be sure to check the *water temperature frequently. You should do it before the experiment, during the experiment, and after the experiment.

2. Today we're going to talk about photosynthesis: how it happens, why it happens, and when it happens.

3. Aesthetic factors, structural factors, and economic factors are all important in architecture.

4. Enthusiastic teachers, well-organized teachers, and knowledgeable teachers usually get the highest ratings.

5. You'll have to collect the sample, identify the sample, and analyze the sample.

☞ **EXERCISE 5.**   With a Partner
            a. Complete each sentence by using a list of at least three members.
            b. Mark the message units with a bar symbol (|).
            c. Mark the primary stress in each message unit with ●.
            d. Read each sentence aloud with a partner.

---

*compound noun

General topics

1. A good TA . . .

2. In order to prevent stress, | you need to . . .

3. Some good topics for *small talk with students are . . .

4. Some things to do on the first day of class are . . .

Personal topics

5. If I had ten million dollars, | I would . . .

6. Four countries I would like to visit are . . .

7. My favorite subjects in *high school were . . .

8. Three important journals in my field are . . .

☛ **EXERCISE 6.**   Academic Terms
a. Write three sentences using a list of at least three members in each. Each sentence should be on a topic in your field of study.
b. Mark the message units with a bar symbol (|).
c. Mark the primary stress in each message unit with ●.
d. Read each sentence aloud with a partner.

Example 1:   Chemistry

An atom is made up of protons, | neutrons, | and electrons.

Example 2:   Civil engineering

When there's an *earthquake, | there are three kinds of *shock waves: |

primary waves, | secondary waves, | and long waves.

---

*compound noun

CHOICE QUESTIONS
AND ANSWERS

☛ **EXERCISE 1.**   a. Listen to the following dialog.

b. Mark the primary stress with ● according to what you hear.

Situation. Two TAs discussing a problem in class

A: What's wrong? Are you worried, | sick, | or just tired?

B: I guess I'm a bit worried. I'm having a problem with two of my students. They're always whispering | while I'm trying to conduct class.

A: Well, are they doing well | or doing poorly?

B: They're doing well. It's just that they're just disturbing me. What do you think? Should I deal with the problem | or ignore it?

A: I think you should deal with it. It's probably bothering the rest of the students, | too.

B: OK. You're right. But should I say something during class | or after class?

A: Probably after class. That way you'll feel less pressure.

Choice Questions

Primary stress and the pitch move go on each alternative in a choice question.

A rise-to-mid-range melody is used on nonfinal choices; a low-range melody is used on the final choice at the end of a sentence.

The Structure of Choice Questions

1. Choice questions begin like *yes/no* questions—with an auxiliary verb or a modal followed by the subject.
2. Each alternative is in a separate message unit. The first may begin with "either." The other phrases may begin with "or," but the last one must begin with "or."

The Sound of Choice Questions

Primary stress. The alternatives themselves are highlighted and therefore receive primary stress. Even though other new information may follow, it is not in focus. The alternatives are in single words. They can be content words (Example 1), or function words (Example 2), or even parts of words (Example 3).

Intonation. Each alternative usually has the rise-to-mid-range melody, except the last one, which has the low-range melody if it is at the end of a sentence. Remember that you can use either the pitch jump or the pitch drop version of each melody pattern.

+---+
| **Answers to Choice Questions** |
| |
| In answers, the primary stress and pitch move are on the element |
| containing the chosen alternative. |
| |
| A low-range melody is used. |
+---+

Example 1:

A: Is that question on the midterm exam | or on the final exam?

B: It's on the midterm exam.

Example 2:

A: Does this beaker go in the cabinet, | under the cabinet, | or on the cabinet?

B: It goes on the cabinet.

Example 3:

        ●   ●

A: Did you study macroeconomics | or microeconomics?

        ●

B: I studied| macroeconomics.

☞ **EXERCISE 2.** a. Divide the choice phrases into message units with a bar
         symbol (|).
        b. Mark the primary stress.
        c. Read the dialogs aloud. T is the teacher, and S is the
         student.

Situation 1. During office hours

 T: I'm glad you came. Let's see . . . are you in the nine o'clock class or the
    eleven o'clock class?

 S: I'm in the eleven o'clock class. I sit by the window.

 T: Oh, yeah. I thought so. Now, did you want to talk about the first assign-
    ment or the second assignment?

 S: The second one. The first one was pretty easy.

Situation 2. Passing out homework

 T: These homework assignments don't have names on them. Is this your
    handwriting or his?

 S: It's not mine. It must be his.

Situation 3. Two TAs discussing their classes

 A: When are you going to give the assignment? Before the quiz or after the
    quiz?

 B: After the quiz. The students will be more relaxed.

Situation 4. Class discussion

    T: Let's look at the exercises on page fifty-nine.

    S: Did you say fifty-nine or sixty-nine?

    T: Oh. Fifty-nine. Did everybody bring their books?

Situation 5. Class discussion

    T: Does the author agree with the theory or disagree with it?

    S: I think she disagrees.

    T: OK. Would you say she strongly disagrees or mildly disagrees?

    S: I guess she just mildly disagrees. She agrees with a small part of it.

Situation 6. During class. (Notice that the answer to T's first question comes in S1's *second* response.)

    T: Would you rather have the quiz on Friday or on Monday?

    S1:   For me, that depends. Is it essay, short answer, multiple choice, or what?

    T: It's going to be multiple choice.

    S1:   Then Friday is OK.

    T: Well, how about the rest of you? Do you prefer Friday, Monday, or even some other day?

    S2:   I think we'll be ready by Friday.

☞ **EXERCISE 3.**   a. Complete the following dialogs with meaningful words and phrases.
    b. Mark the primary stress.
    c. Practice them aloud with a partner.

Situation 1. Checking the homework assignment

    A: Is the homework on page _____ or page _____?

    B: It's on page _____.

Situation 2. Majors

> *A:*   Is your major _____ or _____?
>
> *B:*   It's _____.
>
> *A:*   Oh. Is it easy or hard?
>
> *B:*   It's _____.

Situation 3. Activities before and after class

> *A:*   Do you _____ before this class or after this class?
>
> *B:*   _____ this class. How about you?
>
> *A:*   I _____ _____ this class.

Situation 4. Type of courses

> *A:*   Is _____ a requirement or an elective?
>
> *B:*   It's a(n) _____.

Situation 5. Personal questions

> *A:*   Are you a theorist, a practitioner, or both?
>
> *B:*   I'm _____.
>
> *A:*   Are you a pessimist or an optimist?
>
> *B:*   I'm a(n) _____.
>
> *A:*   Are you a TA or an RA?
>
> *B:*   I'm a(n) _____.

☞ **EXERCISE 4.**   a. With a partner, use the pairs of words below to create meaningful choice question dialogs.
b. Mark the primary stress.
c. Then practice your dialogs aloud with a partner.

　　　　　　　　　　　　●　　　　　　　　●
Example: *A:*   Should we use the same method or a different method?

　　　　　　　　　　　　　　●
　　　　　　B: Let's use a different method this time.

same/different   quantitative research/qualitative research
fact/opinion   textbook/class notes
stimulus/response   specific/general
objective/subjective   empirical evidence/anecdotal evidence
primary/secondary   symmetrical/asymmetrical
deductive reasoning/inductive reasoning
dependent variable/independent variable/random variable

☞ **EXERCISE 5.**   a. Using the pairs of words below, ask your partner about his or her preferences and practices regarding work style.
b. Monitor your use of primary stress.

　　　　　　　　　　　　●　　　　　　　　●
Example: *A:*   Do you prefer a messy desk or a neat desk?

　　　　　　　　　　　　　　●
　　　　　　B: I prefer a messy desk.

messy desk/neat desk   casual/formal
structured/unstructured   high-tech/low-tech
collaborative/competitive   fixed hours/flexible hours
social/private   music/silence

☞ EXERCISE 6.   a. Create two meaningful dialogs using choice questions and answers.
b. Use at least one academic term in each.
c. Mark the primary stress.
d. Practice the dialogs aloud.

Example 1:   Music

A: Is that piece a concerto or a symphony?

B: It's a symphony.

Example 2:   Mathematics

A: Should this be a right triangle or an isosceles triangle?

B: It should be a right triangle.

Example 3:   Statistics

A: Should we cover linear regressions before the break or after the break?

B: In this case, let's do it after the break.

☞ EXERCISE 7.   a. While you are in a class you are taking, write down a choice question and answer that you hear.
b. Mark the primary stress.
c. Repeat the dialog aloud several times.

YES/NO QUESTIONS
AND ANSWERS

☞ **EXERCISE 1.**   a. Listen to the following dialog.
b. Mark the primary stress with ● according to what you
hear.

Situation. Preparing for a biology test. A is the TA.

A: Do you have any questions about next week's test?

B: Yes. Will we have a whole hour?

A: Yes. But I'll collect the tests right at the bell. Is there anything else?

C: Will you be giving any partial credit on the test?

A: I might be. I'll have to talk to the professor about it, | and I'll let you

know. By the way, | you don't have to worry about chromosomes.

D: Why? Aren't they on it?

A: No, they're not. But they'll be on the final.

Yes/No Questions

Primary stress and pitch move go on the last content word in new information or on the last function word if there is no new content word.

The low-range melody or the high-range melody is used.

The Structure of *Yes/No* Questions

1. *Yes/no* questions ask for a positive or negative reply.
2. They have the following structures.

Auxiliary + Subject + Verb + rest of sentence
Do   you   have   any questions about next week's test?
Will   we   have   a whole hour?

Be   + Subject +   rest of sentence
Are   they   on it?

The Sound of *Yes/No* Questions

Primary Stress. *Yes/no* questions simply follow the guideline for primary stress which we are already familiar with.

Intonation. *Yes/no* questions can have either the low-range melody or the high-range melody. Remember that you can use either the pitch jump or the pitch drop version with each melody pattern.

Answers to *Yes/No* Questions

Yes/no questions ask the listener to make a positive or negative reply about the verb. Primary stress and pitch move go on the last content word in the new information or on the last function word if there is no new content word.

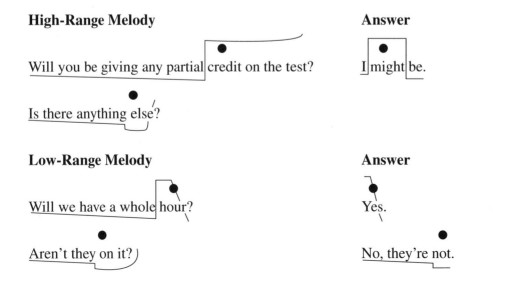

High-Range Melody   **Answer**

Will you be giving any partial credit on the test?   I might be.

Is there anything else?

Low-Range Melody   **Answer**

Will we have a whole hour?   Yes.

Aren't they on it?   No, they're not.

☛ **EXERCISE 2.**   a. In each dialog, mark the primary stress on the last content word in the message unit.
b. Then read the dialogs aloud with a partner.

　　　　　　　　　　　　●
Example: *A:*   Are you busy?

　　　　　　　　●　　　　●
　　　　　B: No. Have a seat.

Situation 1. In a lab

　A: There's something wrong with this microscope.

　B: Is it broken?

　A: I'm not sure.

Situation 2. In class

　A: Are you familiar with the philosophies of Kant?

　B: Not really.

Situation 3. In the office

　A: This is our new *word processor. Do you want to try it?

　B: I don't know. It looks kind of complicated.

Situation 4. Two TAs

　A: Here are the results of Professor Kim's exam. Should I give them to him?

　B: OK. But let's record them first.

Situation 5. Two students

　A: I'm having some problems with my adviser.

　B: Do you want to talk about it?

　A: If you don't mind, | I think it would help.

---

*compound noun

Situation 6. Class review

A: Is the moon a star?

B: No. It doesn't radiate its own light.

A: Is the sun a star?

B: Yes.

Situation 7. Discussing a test

A: Do you think the Psych 104 test is valid?

B: Yes. Our research shows that it's valid.

A: Is it a reliable test?

B: I'm not really sure. We haven't investigated that.

Situation 8. Two undergraduates

A: Wasn't Jeff Byers your TA?

B: Yes. I had him for Bio 110.

A: Was he a good TA?

B: He wasn't bad.

Situation 9. Two TAs in their office

A: What do you think about this *term paper?

B: I think it was plagiarized.

A: I agree. Do you think it was intentionally plagiarized?

B: Well, it's possible.

---

*compound noun

☞ **EXERCISE 3.**   a. In each dialog, mark the primary stress. In the *yes/no* questions, stress the last function word in new information.

b. Then read the dialogs aloud with a partner.

Example 1: *A:* I can't find my calculator. I looked all over my desk.
                                      ●   ●

                 B: Did you look under your desk? I thought I saw it under there.

                 A: Oh. Thanks.

Example 2: *A:* I can't find Professor Simpson. Is he out?

                 B: Yes. He went home sick.

Situation 1. Discussing test results

   A: Look at this curve. It represents the *test results. Is the distribution normal?

   B: No.

   A: OK, why? Should it be normal?

   B: Not necessarily. Our population really wasn't homogeneous.

Situation 2. In the computer lab

   A: I need to use the *laser printer. Is it on?

   B: I don't know. I'll check.

Situation 3. In the office

   A: I'm looking for Dean Curtis. Has she been in?

   B: Well, I just saw her. Let me see if I can find her.

---

*compound noun

Situation 4. Two TAs

A: The student newspaper just published its List of Excellent Teachers.

B: Am I on it?

A: Yes! Congratulations.

Situation 5. Two TAs

A: The new TAs just went to the stacks.

B: Is anyone with them? It's really easy to get lost there.

A: Yes. Professor Morgan's with them.

     REMINDER: Pronouns are typically considered old information unless they are used later to refer to different content.

     ●   ●

A: Where was Elizabeth? Were you with her?

     ●

B: No. I never saw her.   (still the same "her")

     ●   ●

A: I was also looking for Meg. Were you with her?   (a new "her")

B: Yes.

☞ **EXERCISE 4.**   a. In each dialog, mark the primary stress. In the *yes/no* questions, watch especially for pronouns that get new meaning.
                                 b. Then read the dialogs aloud with a partner.

Situation 1. Two TAs

A: There's a *TA meeting at 2:00. Can you be there?

B: Yes. But I don't really want to. I have a feeling it's going to be long. Will you be there?

---

*compound noun

Situation 2. Two TAs

A: I can't teach class this Friday, so I need to find a substitute. Do you have any suggestions?

B: Well, there's Michael Collins. Do you know him?

A: No.

B: Or how about Andy George? Do you know him?

A: Yeah. That's a good idea.

More on Answers to *Yes/No* Questions

1. Often the answer consists of "yes" or "no" plus a short phrase. The phrase usually includes the part of the verb that can be made positive or negative (the auxiliary). In these cases, the new information—and primary stress—is in the verb part that can be made positive or negative: either the first modal or auxiliary or the "not."

   Example: *A:*   Are you going to your office?

                        ●

           B: Yes, I am.

                     ●

          Or   No, I'm not.

2. Sometimes the answer consists of longer phrases that include the original verb—which is now old information. Again, the new information and primary stress fall on the verb part that can be positive or negative: either the first modal or auxiliary or the "not."

   Example 1: *A:*   Are you going to your office?

                     ●   ●

           B: I will be going | as soon as I finish up in the lab.

                        ●   ●

          Or: Well, I should go. But I'm just too busy.

                      ●   ●

          Or: No, I'm not going. I changed my mind.

                                                ●

Example 2:   *A:*   Were you prepared for the pop quiz in physics?

                           ●   ●

           B: I would have been, | but I got sick.

☛ **EXERCISE 5.**   a. In each dialog, mark the primary stress. Pay special attention to the stress on the *answers* to the *yes/no* questions.

                                    b. Then read the dialogs aloud with a partner.

Situation 1. Two students in Asian studies

   A: Do you speak Japanese?

   B: Yes, I do.

Situation 2. Two students studying

   A: Have you finished your paper?

   B: No, I haven't.

Situation 3. Two students after class

   A: Are you ready for your presentation?

   B: Yes, I am.

   A: And are you ready for the quiz?

   B: No, I'm not.

Situation 4. In class

   A: Is three a prime number?

   B: Yes, it is.

   A: Is six a prime number?

   B: No, it isn't.

Situation 5. Discussing research

A: In this experiment, | is the drug the dependent variable?

B: No, it's not. It's the independent variable.

Situation 6. Two TAs

A: Was Tom at the *staff meeting?

B: He should have been. But he wasn't.

Situation 7. Discussing class rosters

A: Was Kevin Taylor one of your students?

B: He might have been. The name sounds familiar.

> NOTE: If you have already covered information questions and answers, you may want to compare the primary stress of answers to *yes/no* questions and answers to information questions (also see Discourse Domains D-13).

●	
A: Who read *Don Quixote?*	(information question)
●	
B: I did.	(Stress the word with the answer.)
●	
A: Did you like it?	(*yes/no* question)
●	
B: Yes, I did.	(Stress the first auxiliary.)
●	
A: Who'll write the *study guide for the quiz?	(information question)
●	
B: I will.	(Stress the word with the answer.)

---

*compound noun

●

But will you help me?   (*yes/no* question)

●

A: Yes, I will.   (Stress the first auxiliary.)

☞ **EXERCISE 6.**   Twenty Questions
a. One member of the class thinks of a noun and tells the other students whether it is an animal, a vegetable, or a mineral.
b. The other students ask *yes/no* questions to try to guess what the noun is.

☞ **EXERCISE 7.**   *Yes/No* Questions for Checking for Understanding
One common use of *yes/no* questions is to check whether the class is keeping up with you. Questions like the ones below can be included at strategic points in your lecture or discussion to give students an opportunity to ask a question or clarify something.
a. Add a few more *yes/no* "checking for understanding" questions on the lines provided below.
b. Mark the stress and read each question aloud.
c. Give a five-minute talk on a topic from your field of study. Include at least two "checking for understanding" questions.

Do you have any questions so far?   Are you following this?

Are you with me?   So far so good?

Does this make sense?   Is there anything you want to ask about?

_____   _____

_____   _____

_____   _____

_____   _____

☞ **EXERCISE 8.**   a. Create two meaningful dialogs that use *yes/no* questions and answers.
    b. Use at least one academic term in each.
    c. Mark the primary stress.
    d. Read the dialogs aloud.

Example 1:   Mathematics

  ●
A: Is this graph concave upward?

    ●   ●
B: No, it isn't. It's concave downward.

Example 2:   Linguistics

  ●
A: Is Basque spoken in Spain?

    ●   ●
B: Yes, it is. But it isn't related to the Spanish language.

☞ **EXERCISE 9.**   a. While you are in a class you are taking, write down a *yes/no* question and answer that you hear.
    b. Mark the primary stress.
    c. Repeat the dialog aloud several times.

D-12

TAG QUESTIONS AND ANSWERS

☛ **EXERCISE 1.** a. Listen to the following dialog.
b. Mark the primary stress with ● according to what you hear.
c. Circle High for the high-range melody or Low for the low-range melody in the *italicized* message units.

Situation. A TA and a student talking after class   **Melody Pattern**

A: I was just looking at your *homework.

You've been having trouble, | *haven't you?*   High   Low

B: Yes, I have.

But I'm not failing the class, | *am I?*   High   Low

A: No, you're not. I was just wondering if you need

any help.

B: Maybe. Your *office hour's at 4:00, | *isn't it?*   High   Low

A: Yes. But you're not free at 4:00, | *are you?*   High   Low

B: Well, I used to have a lab then, | but I dropped it.

So 4:00 is fine.

A: OK. Oh . . . you'll be on time, | *won't you?*   High   Low

I have someone else coming at 4:30.

B: Sure. Thanks a lot.

---

*compound noun

Tag Questions

In the statement portion, primary stress and pitch move go on the last content word in the new information or on the last function word if there is no new content word. In the tag, primary stress goes on the auxiliary.

A high-range melody says that speakers genuinely want the answer ("Tell me!"). A low-range melody says that speakers want agreement with the statement portion ("Agree with me!").

The Structure of Tag Questions

1. Tag questions have at least two message units; they are formed by adding a short question (the "tag") to the end of a statement. The first message unit(s) consist of the statement. The final message unit is the tag. It contains an auxiliary followed by a pronoun, corresponding to the verb and subject of the statement.
2. Notice that if the statement is positive, the auxiliary of the tag is negative. And if the statement is negative, the auxiliary of the tag is positive.

The Sound of Tag Questions

Primary Stress. The change in the auxiliary of the tag—from positive to negative or negative to positive—is the new information. Therefore the auxiliary verb will receive the primary stress and pitch move. The pronoun is old information.

Intonation. Special information is carried in the intonation of tag questions.

The high-range pattern is used when the answer is truly not known; the question asker does not know what the response will be. The melody means "Tell me!"

The low-range pattern is used when the question asker is seeking confirmation of the statement and expects the listener to agree. This melody means "Agree with me!" (Although this melody seems to encourage agreement, the listener is not obligated to agree.)

Remember that a pitch jump version or a pitch drop version can be used with both melody patterns.

Answers to Tag Questions

Primary stress goes on the first auxiliary or the "not."

The low-range melody is used.

●

A: You've been having trouble, |

●   ●

haven't you?   Or: haven't you?   ("Agree with me!")

B: Yes, I have.

●

But I'm not failing the class, |

●   ●

am I?   Or: | am I?   ("Tell me!")

●

A: No, you're not.

☞ **EXERCISE 2.**   a. Mark the primary stress in each message unit with ●.
 b. For the tag questions, circle High for high-range melody and Low for low-range melody. The "Tell me!" and "Agree with me!" clues indicate the speaker's underlying intent.
 c. Read each dialog aloud with a partner.

Situation 1. A TA and a student before class   **Melody**

A: You missed the quiz, | didn't you?   ("Agree with me!")   High   Low

B: Yes, I did. I can make it up, | can't I?   ("Tell me!")   High   Low

A: I don't think so. Let's talk about it

after class.

Situation 2. Two students studying **Melody**

A: It's time for class, | isn't it?	("Agree with me!")	High	Low
B: Yes, it is. You're coming, | aren't you?	("Tell me!")	High	Low
A: I don't know. I'm really swamped.			

Situation 3. A student and a TA

A: Beth, do you know who wrote this poem?			
B: I'm not sure. It wasn't Whitman, | was it?	("Tell me!")	High	Low
A: Yes, it was.			

Situation 4. Two students working on a paper

A: This article isn't very well written, | is it?	("Agree with me!")	High	Low
B: Not really. You're not going to cite it, | are you?	("Tell me!")	High	Low
A: Yes, I am. But I'm going to criticize it.			

Situation 5. Two graduate students

A: How were your prelims? You passed, | didn't you?	("Agree with me!")	High	Low
B: Yes! It's a relief, | isn't it?	("Agree with me!")	High	Low
A: Definitely.			

Situation 6. Two TAs getting ready for class   **Melody**

A: Well, I've finally finished making the

corrections on this handout.

B: You haven't copied it, | have you?   ("Tell me!")   High   Low

A: Why? You don't have another

correction, | do you?   ("Tell me!")   High   Low

B: Well, if it's really not too late.

☞ **EXERCISE 3.**   Tag questions are often used to open a conversation. In
this exercise, practice opening and continuing a conversation.
tion.
a. Based on the following topics, write down a tag question to ask a classmate.
tion to ask a classmate.
b. Mark the primary stress.
c. Ask the classmate your question.
d. Continue the conversation for at least one more turn by commenting on your classmate's answer or asking another question.
other question.

Example 1:   *A:*   You speak Spanish, | don't you?

B: Actually, I don't. But I've visited Peru.

A: Oh! It's beautiful, | isn't it?

B: Yes, it is.

Example 2:   *A:*   You're not new to campus, | are you?

B: No, I'm not. But you're new, | aren't you?

A: Yes, I am. I just arrived last month.

B: How do you like it?

Possible topics

office hours	teaching assistantship
native country	likes classical/rock/country music
field of study	happy/bored/tired/etc.
rides bus/bike to class	knows _____ (some mutual friend)
new to campus this semester	speaks _____ (Spanish, Hindi, etc.)

☞ **EXERCISE 4.** Tag Questions in Discussing Opinions
  a. View a videotape of a TA teaching a class.
  b. Based on what you saw on the videotape, write down a tag question to ask a classmate.
  c. Mark the primary stress.
  d. After watching the tape, ask the classmate your question.
  e. Continue the conversation for at least one more turn by commenting on your classmate's answer or asking another question.

　　　　　　　　● 　 ●
Examples:　He spoke really clearly, | didn't he?

　　　　　　　　　　● 　 ●
　　　　His writing was hard to read, | wasn't it?

☞ **EXERCISE 5.** a. Create two meaningful dialogs using tag questions and answers.
  b. Use at least one academic term in each.
  c. Mark the message units and primary stress.
  d. Practice the dialogs aloud with a partner.

Example 1:　Statistics

　　　　　　　　● 　 ●
　A:　We need to compute the correlation, | don't we?

　　　　　● 　　　　　　● 　　　　　　●
　B:　Yes, we do. It should be a rank-difference correlation, | shouldn't it?

　　　● 　　　　　●
　A:　Right. The Spearman rho.

Example 2:   Biology lab

                ●   ●

A: This isn't an artery, | is it?

                ●   ●

B: No, it isn't. It's a vein.

☛ **EXERCISE 6.**   a. While you are in a class you are taking, write down a tag question and answer that you hear.
b. Mark the primary stress.
c. Repeat the dialog aloud several times.

D-13

INFORMATION QUESTIONS
AND ANSWERS

☞ **EXERCISE 1.**   a. Listen to the following dialog.
 b. Mark the primary stress with ● according to what you hear.

Situation. Discussing a homework problem. A is the TA. The others are students.

A: Why don't we get started? Let's go over the homework. Number one. Ben, what did you get for the answer?

B: I got 89.

A: OK. Who got a different answer?

C: I did.

A: What did you get?

C: I got 85.

D: How can this be? I got something completely different!

A: Really? What was it?

D: 374. So who has the right answer?

A: I have it. But let's work it out together.

Information Questions

Primary stress and the pitch move go on the last content word in new information or on the last function word if there is no new content word.

Information questions usually have a low-range melody.

The Structure of Information Questions

1. Information questions ask for information about something by using a question word or phrase, such as *who, what, where, when, why, how, how much,* etc.

2. Information questions typically have the following structures.

Question word   +   Auxiliary   +   Subject   +   Verb
Why   don't   we   get started?

Question word   +   Verb   +   rest of sentence
for the subject
Who   got   a different answer?

The Sound of Information Questions

Primary Stress. The stress of information questions follows patterns we are already familiar with.

Intonation. Information questions use a low-range melody. Remember that you can use either the pitch jump version or the pitch drop version.

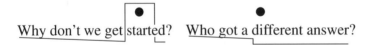

Why don't we get started?   Who got a different answer?

Answers to Information Questions

The answer to the question is in focus—the answer is the new information. It can be a content word or a function word.

The low-range melody is used.

Example 1:   *A:*   How are you?

          B: I'm fine. ("Fine" answers "How?")

Example 2:   *A:*   Who wrote *War and Peace*?

          B: Tolstoy wrote it. ("Tolstoy" answers "Who?")

Example 3:   *A:*   Whose disk is this? I found it on my desk.

●

        B: <u>I think it's my disk</u>. I must have left it there. ("My" answers

"Whose?")

☞ **EXERCISE 2.**   a. Mark the primary stress in the following dialogs, using
      ● on the last content word in new information.
    b. Then read the dialogs aloud with a partner.

Example:

          ●

Student A: When's the final?
TA: It's on December 5th. We're going to have a *review session on
    Friday.

          ●

Student B: What'll be covered on the final?
TA: Everything. But most of it is on macroeconomic theory.

Situation 1. Classroom questions

TA: What's the first step in the scientific method?

Student A: Defining the problem.

TA: Right. What's the second step?

Student B: Researching the topic.

Situation 2. A geology class

TA: Where can we find sulfur?

Student A: It's found in meteorites.

TA: Yes. What are some characteristics of sulfur?

Student B: It's a pale yellow solid.

Situation 3. A physics class

TA:	How do we measure force?
Student A:	It's measured by the rate of change of momentum.
TA:	OK. So how do we calculate force?
Student B:	You multiply mass by acceleration.

Situation 4. A statistics class

TA:	What's represented on the horizontal axis?
Student A:	The students' *test scores.
TA:	And what's on the vertical axis?
Student B:	The number of students.

☛ **EXERCISE 3.**   a. Mark the primary stress in the dialogs. In the information questions, stress the last function word in new information.
b. Then read the dialogs aloud with a partner.

Example:

                                        ●   ●
A: Don't forget about the *review session. It's tonight at 7:30.

                    ●
B: Where'll it be?

                        ●
A: In 293 Lincoln Hall.

Situation 1. In the lab

A: I just got a new probe. Do you want to see it?

B: What's it for?

A: It's for my research in NMR spectroscopy.

---

*compound noun

Situation 2. Planning a quiz

> *A:*   We need to schedule one more quiz. When should it be?
>
> *B:*   How about next Friday?

Situation 3. Class discussion

> *TA:*   What were the subjects' symptoms before administering the drug?
>
> *Student A:*   Headaches and high *blood pressure.
>
> *TA:*   OK. What were the subjects' symptoms after administering it?
>
> *Student B:*   There really was no significant change.

Situation 4. Planning a meeting

> *TA:*   I'd like you to stop by my office. I think we need to talk about
>   your quiz.
>
> *Student:*   Well, OK. Where is your office?
>
> *TA:*   It's in Roger Adams Lab, | on the third floor.
>
>   REMINDER: Pronouns and other proforms are typically considered old
>   information.

Situation 5. In the lab

> *A:*   Look at the slide in this microscope. What do you think?
>
> *B:*   I don't know. What is it?
>
> *A:*   I think it's a *cancer cell.

Situation 6. Missing keys

> *A:*   Do you have the keys to the *computer room?
>
> *B:*   Yes. I thought I had lost them.
>
> *A:*   Where were they?
>
> *B:*   They were in my desk.

---

*compound noun

REMINDER: Pronouns and other proforms are considered new information if they are used again to refer to new content.

A: Don't forget about our *TA meeting.

●

B: Oh, yeah. When do we have to be there?   ("There" is old.)

A: At three-thirty. Then there's our *group meeting.

●

B: When do we have to be there?   (a new "there")

A: It's at five.

☞ **EXERCISE 4.**   a. Mark the primary stress in the following dialogs. Watch especially for pronouns that get new meaning.
　　　　　　　　　　b. Then read the dialogs aloud with a partner.

Example:

●

A: What did you get on your test?

●　　　　　　　●

B: I got an 89. What did you get?

●　　　　　　　●

A: I got a 78. And I feel pretty lucky about it.

Situation 1. A literature class

TA: Dante was a significant author in the Middle Ages. What did he write?

Student A: *The Divine Comedy.*

TA: Right. And Chaucer was another significant author. What did he write?

Student B: *The *Canterbury Tales.*

---

*compound noun

Situation 2. A forestry class

TA: What kind of tree is this?

Student A: It's a silver maple.

TA: Good. Let's look at another one. What kind of tree is this?

Student B: It's a red maple.

☞ **EXERCISE 5.**   a. Mark the primary stress in the following dialogs, using
●. Pay careful attention to the stress on the answers.
b. Then read the dialogs aloud with a partner.

Example:

●
A: What kind of rock is this?

●
B: It's an igneous rock.

Situation 1. A chemistry class

TA: How many isotopes of sodium do scientists recognize?

Student: I think there are seven isotopes.

Situation 2. An economics class

A: According to the graph, | which occupation employs the highest percent-
age of women?

B: Clerical occupations.

A: Right. And which occupation employs the lowest percentage of women?

B: Mechanical occupations.

Situation 3. A business class

A: How much did company A increase in sales?

B: By about 12 percent.

A: And how much did company B increase in sales?

B: Around 40 percent. They had a bigger *advertising budget.

Situation 4. After class

A: Whose book is that?

B: Oh. It's yours. I guess I picked it up by mistake.

Situation 5. In the office

A: A book just arrived in the mail.

B: Who's it for?

A: It's for you.

Situation 6. Planning the lab

A: Who's going to set up the lab?

B: I'll do it. It's my turn.

> NOTE: Compare the primary stress of answers to information questions and answers to *yes/no* questions (also see Discourse Domains D-11).

A: Who's going to tell the professor what we think?   (information question)

      ●

B: I am.   (Stress the word with the answer.)

A: Are you sure?   (*yes/no* question)

        ●

B: Yes, I am.   (Stress the first auxiliary.)

---

*compound noun

A: Who can write the quiz?   (information question)

      ●

B: I can.   (Stress the word with the answer.)

A: Great. Can you write the *answer key, too?   (*yes/no* question)

      ●

B: Yes, I can.   (Stress the first auxiliary.)

☞ **EXERCISE 6.**   a. Complete the following dialogs with your own expressions.

                        b. Mark the primary stress in the following dialogs, using ●.

                        c. Then read the dialogs aloud with a partner.

A: What are you studying?

B: I'm studying _____. What are you studying?

A: _____.

A: When's your next class?

B: It's _____. When's your next class?

A: It's _____.

A: Where do you usually study?

B: I usually study _____. Where do you study?

A: _____.

☞ **EXERCISE 7.**   a. Write down three information questions that you would ask a current TA in your department.

                        b. Mark the primary stress.

                        c. Practice the questions aloud with a partner in class.

                        d. Then ask the TA the questions you practiced. Your instructor can help you with ways to initiate the conversation.

---

*compound noun

☞ EXERCISE 8. a. Study the following table.
b. Write down three information questions you could ask a class about the table.
c. Mark the primary stress.
d. Practice asking and answering the questions with a partner.

Participation in National Elections

Country	1985		1995	
	Persons of Voting Age (millions)	Percentage Voted	Persons of Voting Age (millions)	Percentage Voted
Country A	125	72	142	68
Country B	98	81	84	81
Country C	72	82	75	84

☞ EXERCISE 9. a. Write two meaningful dialogs that include at least one information question and answer in each.
b. Use at least one academic term in each.
c. Mark the primary stress.
d. Read the dialogs aloud.

Example:

TA: What is *Grave's disease?

Student A: It's a disease of the thyroid.

TA: Yes. What are some symptoms of Grave's disease?

Student B: *Weight loss and emotional disturbance.

---

*compound noun

☛ **EXERCISE 10.** a. While you are in a class you are taking, write down two information questions and answers that you hear.

b. Mark the primary stress.

c. Read each dialog aloud several times.

D-14

NARROWED QUESTIONS
AND ANSWERS

☞ **EXERCISE 1.** Listen to the following dialog and mark the primary stress with ● according to what you hear. A is the teacher, and the others are students.

A: Who wrote the *Communist Manifesto*?

B: Karl Marx.

A: Right. When did he write it?

C: I think it was in the 1800s.

A: Yes. . . . When in the 1800s?

C: The middle 1800s. I think it was 1848.

A: Exactly. Why did he write it?

D: He was calling on the masses to revolt against their economic conditions.

A: Right. And we can come back to that later. What else did he write?

B: *Das Kapital.*

Narrowed Questions

Primary stress and pitch move go on the question word or phrase.

A low-range melody is used.

The Purpose and Structure of Narrowed Questions

In the classroom, instructors often ask related questions. **Narrowed questions** focus on the content of a previous question or statement by asking for more specific information. Grammatically, they are formed like information questions, but they sound different.

The Sound of Narrowed Questions

Primary Stress. Our familiar primary stress rule applies to narrowed questions. The new information is in the question word or phrase; the other words are old information. So the primary stress and pitch jump occur on the question word or phrase. After the primary stress, remember to keep your voice at a low, quiet pitch.

Intonation. The low-range melody is used. Remember that you can use either the pitch jump version or the pitch drop version.

Answers to Narrowed Questions

Primary stress and pitch move go on the last content word in the new information or on the last function word if there is no new content word.

A low-range melody is used.

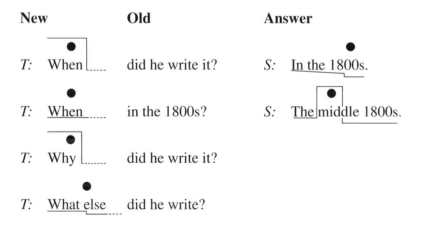

New	Old	Answer
T: When —	did he write it?	*S:* In the 1800s.
T: When —	in the 1800s?	*S:* The middle 1800s.
T: Why —	did he write it?	
T: What else —	did he write?	

NOTE 1: All question words can be used in narrowed questions.

> *who   what   where   when   why   how   which*

Narrowed questions also frequently have question phrases. These are stressed on the last part of the phrase (unlike repetition questions). Some common ones are the following.

What else	How much	What type	At what point
Who else	How many	What kind	At what time
(etc.)		What sort	

NOTE 2: The use of narrowed questions is determined by context. Compare (T is the teacher; S is the student)

Dialog A	**Dialog B**
T: What did company A spend most of its money on?	*T:* How much did company A spend on advertising?
S: On research.	*S:* About 12 percent of its budget.
●	*T:* *How much did it spend on*
T: *How much did it spend on research?*	●
S: About 30 percent of its budget.	*research?*
	S: About 30 percent.

While the italicized questions have the same written form, the context and the stress distinguish them for the listener. Dialog A contains a narrowed question; it asks for more detail on the topic of money. Dialog B does not. It goes on to a new topic, research.

☛ **EXERCISE 2.**   In the dialogs below,
a. Mark the primary stress on each message unit using ●.
b. Read the dialogs aloud with a partner.

Situation 1. A class on measurement and evaluation

T: Does anybody see any problems with this research?

S: I think there are some problems with validity.

T: OK. What type of validity?

S: Internal validity.

T: Good. What kind of internal validity?

S: I think it's called *test effect.

---

*compound noun

Situation 2. A student comes to the instructor during office hours

S: I'm having some problems with the assignment.

T: Which assignment?

S: The one on page 96.

T: OK. What kinds of problems?

S: I can't figure out the area of the trapezoid.

Situation 3. Teacher and graduate student discussing their research

T: I found some really good references for our proposal in the library.

S: Oh yeah? Which library?

T: In the public library.

S: Great. I have to go there today anyway. Where in the library?

T: On the lower level—toward the back.

Situation 4. Students from the same class discussing an assignment

S1: When do we need to turn in the first paper?

S2: I think it's due sometime in March.

S1: When in March?

S2: Let me check the syllabus. . . . The third week.

S3: Oh no! The same week as my *physics test. When in the third week?

S2: On the twenty-fourth. That's a Tuesday.

REMINDER

- A narrowed question is defined by context. It is signaled by primary stress on the question word or phrase, as in Dialog A, and by falling intonation.

---

*compound noun

- While the italicized question in Dialog C contains old information near the end and functions similarly to a narrowed question, it is still simply an information question because it goes on to a new topic, spending.

Dialog A

T: What did company A spend most of its money on?

S: On research.

●

T: *How much did it spend on research?*

S: About 30 percent of its budget.

Dialog C

T: How much did company A allot for research?

S: About 12 percent of its budget.

●

T: *How much did it spend on research?*

S: About 30 percent.

☞ **EXERCISE 3.**   a. Identify each question as a narrowed question or an information question.
   b. Mark the primary stress on each message unit in the dialog.
   c. Read each dialog aloud with a partner.

Example:

●

_____Info Q_____   *T:* What did company A spend most of its money on?

●

S: On research.

●

__Narrowed Q__   *T:* How much did it spend on research?

●

S: About 30 percent of its budget.

●

____Info Q____   *T:* How much did it allot for research?

●

S: About 12 percent.

Situation 1. Class discussion

_____   *T:*   In this study, | what happened to the first group of subjects?

                    S: Their scores increased.

_____   *T:*   What happened to the second group of subjects?

                    S: Their scores stayed the same.

_____   *T:*   Why did they stay the same?

                    S: Maybe because they didn't have as much exposure to the stimulus.

Situation 2. Class discussion

_____   *T:*   Who agrees with the author's conclusion?

                      ●

                    S1:   I do. (For an explanation of this stress pattern, see Discourse Domain D-13: Information Questions and Answers.)

_____   *T:*   Who else agrees?

                    S2:   I agree, | too.

_____   *T:*   Who disagrees with the conclusion?

                    S3:   I do.

_____   *T:*   Why do you disagree?

                    S3:   There isn't enough evidence to support it.

☛ **EXERCISE 4.**   With a Partner
a. Complete the following four dialogs.
b. Mark the primary stress.
c. Practice the dialogs aloud.

A: Where are you from?	*A:* What's your major?
B: I'm from _____ (country).	*B:* It's _____.
A: Where in _____ (country)?	*A:* What area of _____?
B: _____ (city).	*B:* _____.

A: When will you finish your degree?

B: In _____ (year).

A: When in _____ (year)?

B: In _____ (month), I hope.

A: Where is your next class?

B: In _____
(building).

A: Where in _____
(building)?

B: In room #_____.

☛ **EXERCISE 5.**   Asking Questions about a Table

      a. Study the table below.

      b. Write down one question you could ask a class about the table. Then write down a narrowed question that could follow up your first question.

      c. Mark the primary stress of each question.

      d. Practice asking and answering the questions with a partner.

Numbers of Students in Different Majors at XYZ College

Majors	Freshmen	Sophomores	Juniors	Seniors
Hard sciences	1,500	1,400	1,250	1,200
Business	1,500	1,550	1,550	1,550
Engineering	1,000	1,000	1,100	1,100
Humanities	550	600	650	700
Other	450	450	450	450

☞ **EXERCISE 6.**   In Your Own Words

a. Construct three short dialogs of your own that contain at least one narrowed question and at least one general or specific academic term. Try to use a classroom or lab situation.

b. Mark the primary stress of each phrase.

c. Read the dialogs aloud.

Example 1:   Computers

T: If you want to run this *application program, you're going to need some

●

additional RAM.

●

S: How much additional RAM?

●

T: About two more megabytes.

Example 2:   Biology

●   ●

T: Think about this example. Plants like beans and peas | receive fixed nitro-

●   ●

gen from the bacterium *Rhizobium.* In return, | the plant supplies *Rhizo-*

●   ●

bium with an *energy source. What is this phenomenon called?

●

S: Symbiosis.

●   ●

T: Right. What kind of symbiosis?

●

S: Mutualism.

---

*compound noun

☛ **EXERCISE 7.**   In a class you are taking, listen for a narrowed question.
a. Identify a narrowed question you hear.
b. Write down the question and answer that came before it.
c. Write down the narrowed question and the answer and mark the primary stress.

Example:

T: Look at our graph. In the *short run, variable factors are added to fixed factors. What eventually happens to the amount of marginal product? (question before)

S: It diminishes. (answer before)

●

T: That's right. At what point does it diminish? (narrowed question)

●

S: When you add the third worker to the *production setting. (answer)

---

*compound noun

D-15

REPETITION QUESTIONS
AND ANSWERS

☛ **EXERCISE 1.**   a. Listen to the following dialog.
                      b. Mark the primary stress according to what you hear.

Situation. A TA (A) leading a discussion in a noisy building

A: It's pretty noisy out in the hall, | but let's start our review, | because the quiz is on Tuesday.

B: When's the quiz?

A: On Tuesday. I guess I need to talk louder. OK, last time we were talking about Hernando Cortés. Now, what did he do?

B: He conquered the Incas.

A: He conquered the Incas?

B: No—wait. The Aztecs.

A: Right. The Aztecs. It was in Mexico. Does anyone remember what year this was?

C: 1519.

A: Sorry, I can't hear you. Did you say 1519?

C: Yeah.

A: Excellent. 1519.

> ## Repetition Questions
>
> Repetition questions ask the listener to repeat or reconsider some information already given.
>
> Repetition questions can be a form of information questions (but stressed on the question word) or statement questions or *yes/no* questions (but stressed on the last unclear or challenged word).
>
> Repetition questions have a high-range melody.

The Purpose of Repetition Questions

Repetition questions are very useful in the classroom. They perform a variety of functions.

- Asking for repetition of some unclear information: "When's the quiz?"
- Repeating some information to check for understanding: "You said 1519?"
- Repeating some information to challenge or question its truth: "The Incas?"

  Many instructors use this structure when a student gives a wrong answer, because it signals to the student to reconsider the response.

- Reviewing material: "What did he do?"

  On questions for review, it is also possible to use the stress of information questions. For example, in this case, you can also put the primary stress on "do." However, using the stress and intonation of repetition questions directly implies that the information was covered earlier in the class.

The Structure of Repetition Questions

In structure, repetition questions can look like information questions, *yes/no* questions, or statement questions. In many cases, the question is not in full form.

- Information question structure

Full form:	"When's the quiz?" Or: "When is it?"
Abbreviated:	"When?"

- *Yes/no* question structure

  Full form: "Did you say 1519?"
  Abbreviated: "1519?"

- Statement question structure

  Full form: "He conquered the Incas?"
  Abbreviated: "The Incas?"

The Sound of Repetition Questions

Intonation. Repetition questions always have a high-range melody. Remember that you can use either the pitch jump version or the pitch drop version.

Primary Stress. In repetition questions, the focus is on the unknown or unclear information. This is what attracts primary stress.

- **Information Question Structure.** Primary stress and pitch move are on the question word (which stands for the unclear word or phrase).

  When's the quiz?

  Notice that, unlike narrowed questions, even if the question element is a phrase ("how much," "what kind," "who else," etc.), the primary stress and pitch move are on the question word itself.

  A: This question will be worth ten points.

  B: How many points?

  A: Ten.

- *Yes/No* **Question Structure and Statement Question Structure.** Primary stress goes on the last content word that is unclear or challenged. In this example, even though "1519" has been said before, it is back in focus because it is the unclear element.

  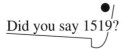

  Did you say 1519?

> ### Answers to Repetition Questions
>
> In answers to repetition questions, the focus is on the answer to the question.
>
> Primary stress and pitch move go on the last content word in the new information or on the last function word if there is no new content word.

☞ **EXERCISE 2.**   a. Use the context in the following dialogs to identify repetition questions. Then write RQ after them.
b. Mark the primary stress.
c. Read the dialogs aloud with a partner, remembering to use a high-range melody on the repetition questions. T is the teacher, and S is the student.

Example 1:   In biology class

T: OK, last time we talked about photosynthesis, so let's review. Now, what did we call the pigment?   *RQ*

S1:   Chlorophyll.

T: Yes, chlorophyll. And what does it do?   *RQ*

S2:   It traps the energy required to split the water.

T: Right.

Example 2:   In statistics class

T: Let's calculate the standard deviation of this set of scores. What should we do first?

S: We need to find the median.

T: The median?   *RQ*

S: No—wait. The mean.

Situation 1. Going over homework

T: What is the answer to problem #12?

S: Forty pounds.

T: Forty?

S: I think so. Oh, I guess it's fifty.

T: Right. Fifty. How did you get that?

Situation 2. During a discussion section

T: Everybody, let's take a look at the book | for an example of a *regression analysis.

S: Which page?

T: Page 45.

S: Which page?

T: Page 45. It's near the end of chapter 2.

Situation 3. A computer science class

T: OK, let's review. Yesterday, we talked about two different types of *programming loops. Now, what were the two types?

S: *"Do-loops" and *"while-loops."

T: Yes, that's right. And which one do we need in problem #7?

S: Do-loops.

T: Did you say do-loops?

S: Yes.

---

*compound noun

Situation 4. Some students talking

A: Dana, Jeff, and I are getting together tonight at Ben's to study for the final. Do you want to join us?

B: Maybe. What are you going to cover?

A: We're going to concentrate on the last four chapters of the book.

B: OK, I'll try to make it. Let me write this down. Now, when is it?

A: Tonight. We're probably going to start around 7:30.

B: And where?

A: At Ben's. Do you know where he lives?

B: Ben? Yeah. But I'll need a ride. Who else is going?

A: Dana and Jeff.

B: Great. I'll call them. Thanks.

☛ **EXERCISE 3.**   a. Complete the following dialogs.
b. Identify repetition questions by writing RQ after them.
c. Mark the primary stress.
d. Read the dialogs aloud with a partner, remembering to use a high-range melody on the repetition questions.

A: I've never studied _____.

B: Did you say _____?

A: _____.

A: When are your *office hours?

B: They're _____.

A: When are they?

B: _____.

---

*compound noun

A: After class I'm going to _____.

B: You're going to _____?

A: _____.

A: My next class is in _____.

B: Where?

A: In _____.

☞ **EXERCISE 4.**   Role Plays with Repetition Questions
   a. You are new to your department, and you are meeting new TAs at a very noisy party.
   b. With a partner, take turns asking each other questions and repeating information to check for understanding. Use the topics provided if you wish.
   c. Do the role play with a partner, monitoring your stress and intonation on the repetition questions.

●

Example: *A:*   What do you think of the department?

●

   B: I think it's really good.

●

   A: What do you think of it?

●

   B: I said it's really good.

Possible topics

the quality of the department   the professors in the department
the opportunities for research   the *office space
the curriculum   the access to computers

---

*compound noun

☛ **EXERCISE 5.**   a. Write four dialogs. Each one should use a repetition question with a different purpose.
- Asking for repetition of unclear information
- Repeating information to check for understanding
- Repeating information to challenge its accuracy
- Reviewing information previously discussed

b. Use at least one academic term in each dialog.
c. Mark the primary stress.
d. Read the dialogs aloud with a partner, remembering to use a high-range melody on the repetition questions.

Example 1:   Astronomy
Asking for repetition of unclear information

A: Most asteroids orbit between Mars and Jupiter.

B: Between where?

A: Between Mars and Jupiter.

Example 2:   Economics
Repeating information to check for understanding

A: Some costs of production fluctuate directly with changes in the amount of

production or the amount of sales. This is called variable cost.

B: Variable?

A: Yes, variable. It varies according to how much you sell or produce.

Example 3:   Mathematics
Repeating information to challenge its accuracy

A: In this diagram, how long is the *line segment connecting point A to point B?

B: It's four centimeters.

*compound noun

●   ●   ●
A: Four? A to B, | not A to C.

●   ●
B: Oh. It's eight centimeters.

● ●
A: Yes. Eight.

Example 4:   U.S. History
Reviewing information previously discussed

               ●   ●
A: Friday we started looking at the *Monroe Doctrine. What did it say?

                                            ●
B: It opposed allowing Europe to extend its influence in the Western Hemisphere.

☛ **EXERCISE 6.**   a. While you are in a class you are taking, write down one repetition question you hear and its answer.
b. Identify its purpose.
     • Asking for repetition of unclear information
     • Repeating information to check for understanding
     • Repeating information to challenge its accuracy
     • Reviewing information previously discussed
c. Mark the primary stress.
d. Read the dialog aloud several times.

---

*compound noun

WORD STRESS DOMAINS

This workbook provides practice and review materials for the word stress rules presented in the Patterns sections of units W-5–W-8 in *Speechcraft*'s core text. For each word stress rule, the Patterns should be completed before doing the Practice and Review sections. Also included here are units on construction stress.

KEY STRESS RULE:
PRACTICE AND REVIEW

W-5A. Final Key Rule Endings *-ion, -iate, -ial,* etc.

PRACTICE

☛ **EXERCISE 1.**   Key Stress Rule Words in Context
a. Identify Key Stress Rule words in items 1–7.
b. Mark the stress of each word.
c. Read each sentence or phrase aloud.
d. Observe a TA during office hours (live or videotaped) and write down the language the TA uses to accomplish two of these strategies.

Language Functions of TAs during Office Hours

Research has shown that TAs typically use the following strategies when working with individual students during office hours.

1. Consciously listening to students' problems.

2. Asking a series of questions in order to arrive at an evaluation of a problem and to break it down into manageable steps.

3. Leading the students to actively engage in solving equations or reaching conclusions, rather than providing answers directly.

4. Giving students permission to ask many questions and responding to them appropriately.

5. Responding to rather than initiating topics for discussion.

6. Providing correction directly rather than indirectly.

7. Controlling the degree of information that students have about upcoming examinations.

☞ **EXERCISE 2.**   In items 1–8 below,
  a. Mark the stress of each Key Stress Rule word.
  b. Read each sentence or phrase aloud.
  c. Observe a lab TA and record the language he or she uses for two of the items.

Language Functions of Lab TAs

Research has shown that TAs in science labs typically use language for the following functions.

1. Give a brief introduction to the lab: Why we are doing today's experiment.

2. Give the essential information students need in order to do the lab but not unnecessary details.

3. Give clear directions to the group and to individuals.

4. Circulate—make a conscious effort to check on all students.

5. Make revisions in explanations when something is wrong or unclear.

6. Use direct language for crucial instructions ("Never touch that") and safety precautions.

7. Providing words of assurance to students who may be anxious about their progress ("That region looks fine").

8. Offering congratulations and praise when something turns out right ("Oh, the spectra are really nice").

☛ **EXERCISE 3.**   Key Stress Rule Words in Context: Making an Announcement
   a. Identify Key Stress Rule words and mark their stress.
   b. Read each sentence or phrase aloud.
   c. Imagine that you are going to explain the new policy on capricious grading to your students. Use the information below and give an extemporary announcement.

New Policy on Capricious Grading

Definition: Giving a grade based on criteria other than those initially established in the course.

New procedure: Students must submit their allegations, with the essential evidence, in writing to the Capricious Grading Committee. A copy should be sent to the instructor of the course. The instructor is required to provide a written reaction to the committee within two weeks.

For further information: Contact the Office of Student Affairs in the Henry Administration Building.

REVIEW

Key Stress Rule

For words with key rule endings, stress the key syllable.

☛ **EXERCISE 1.**   General Academic Terms
a. Write down your general academic terms that have key rule endings.
b. Mark the stress.
c. Read each word aloud.

_____   _____   _____

_____   _____   _____

_____   _____   _____

_____   _____   _____

_____   _____   _____

☛ **EXERCISE 2.**   Specific Academic Terms
a. Write down your specific academic terms that have key rule endings.
b. Mark the stress.
c. Read each word aloud.

_____   _____   _____

_____   _____   _____

_____   _____   _____

_____   _____   _____

_____   _____   _____

☛ **EXERCISE 3.**   Write two dialogs and two short passages.

    a. In each use at least one Key Stress Rule general academic term and one Key Stress Rule specific academic term.

    b. Mark the stress of the Key Stress Rule words.

    c. Read the dialogs and short passages aloud.

Examples:

Statistics

    This graph shows a biváriate distribútion, and we're going to try to find the regréssion line, or the line of best fit. One thing that will help us do that is Pearson's least-squares critérion. Can anyone remember the definítion?

Rhetoric

A: What do you think about the argumentátion in this article?

B: There isn't suffícient evidence to justify his conclúsions.

W-5B. Nonfinal Key Rule Endings
-ional, -iary, etc.

PRACTICE

☛ **EXERCISE 1.**   In the questions below,
         a. Identify Key Stress Rule words and mark their stress.
         b. Read the questions aloud.

1. Do you prefer to take the initiative or to follow others' plans?
2. Who is a revolutionary figure in your native country?
3. What are the advantages and disadvantages of being a perfectionist?
4. Do you know any colloquialisms in English?
5. What are some topics that are considered unmentionable in *small talk?
6. Are instructional practices in your country different from those in the United States?
7. Do you feel appreciative when someone corrects your English?
8. Is there a disproportionate number of either men or women in your department?
9. Do you favor a more traditional style or a more unconventional style of clothing?
10. If someone disagrees with you, are you usually conciliatory or retaliatory?
11. What does it mean to overspecialize in an academic area? Give an example from your own academic field.
12. How is plagiarism defined on your campus?
13. Do you consider yourself a practitioner or a theoretician?
14. How do people rationalize cheating on exams or homework?
15. Have you ever been the beneficiary of good advice? What was it?
16. What are the characteristics of a good conversationalist?

☛ **EXERCISE 2.**   With a partner, ask and answer the questions in Exercise 1.

*compound noun

REVIEW

Key Stress Rule

For words with **key rule endings,** stress the **key syllable.**

Nonbasic Endings following Key Rule Endings

Set 1

-er	*-ive*
execútioner	appréciative

Set 2

-al	*-able*	*-ate*
proféssional	fáshionable	disórientate

Set 3

-y	*-ary*	*-ory*
intermédiary	vísionary	concíliatory

Set 4

-ize	*-ist*	*-ism*
famíliarize	impérialist	creátionism

Set 5

-alize	*-alist*	*-alism*
rátionalize	rátionalist	rátionalism

☛ **EXERCISE 1.**   General Academic Terms

a. Write down your general academic terms that have nonbasic endings following key rule endings.

b. Mark the stress.

c. Read each word aloud.

_____   _____   _____

_____   _____   _____

_____   _____   _____

_____   _____   _____

_____   _____   _____

☛ **EXERCISE 2.**   Specific Academic Terms
a. Write down your specific academic terms that have nonbasic endings following key rule endings.
b. Mark the stress.
c. Read each word aloud.

_____	_____	_____
_____	_____	_____
_____	_____	_____
_____	_____	_____
_____	_____	_____

☛ **EXERCISE 3.**   Write two short dialogs and two short passages.
a. In each use at least one Key Stress Rule general academic term or one Key Stress Rule specific academic term with nonfinal key rule endings.
b. Mark the stress of the Key Stress Rule words.
c. Read the dialogs and short passages aloud.

Examples:

Religious Studies

Many relígionists are now challenging the tradítional Chrístian definí-tion of a míssionary as one who takes the gospel, or the Chrístian story of redémption, to people of a different cultural background.

U.S. History

A: We need to refamíliarize ourselves with the movements leading up to the Civil War. Does anyone remember any of these?
B: Well, I think one of them was called abolítionism.
A: Yes. We had the abolítionists. Now, how did the South respond to them?
C: Wasn't there a secéssionist movement?
A: Right. The South wanted to leave the Únion.

V/VC Stress Rule: Practice and Review

W-6A. V/VC Rule Endings *-al, -ous, ic*

Practice

☛ **EXERCISE 1.** In the dialogs below,
a. Identify, analyze, and mark the stress on V/VC Stress Rule words.
b. Read the dialogs aloud.

Situation 1. Two graduate students talking

A: Do you think this *journal article is too theoretical?

B: Well, according to an anonymous reviewer, it needs to have more practical applications.

A: It could also use some more experimental evidence.

Situation 2. A TA and a student after class

Student: Since this class is so informal, I thought you would be more generous with the grades.

Teacher: Well, I've explained my *grading system in the syllabus.

Student: I just think you've been too rigorous on the first exam.

Teacher: Let's see. Could you show me specifically where you think I was too critical?

---

*compound noun

Situation 3. Two classmates talking

A: How do you like your *economics class?

B: It's really monotonous. And the textbook is archaic!

A: Are you going to drop it?

B: Probably. The whole thing is so ridiculous.

Situation 4. A TA and a student during office hours

Student: I need to talk to you about my paper on ethics. Can you tell me why I got a C?

Teacher: Your ideas were really original. But there were numerous structural problems.

Student: I know I had some circuitous explanations.

☞ **EXERCISE 2.**   In the readings below,
a. Identify, analyze, and mark the stress on V/VC Stress Rule words.
b. Read the passages aloud.
c. Think of two or three questions to ask regarding each passage. Ask them to a partner and discuss the answers.

Reading 1

Nonverbal behavior has a tremendous effect on any oral message, and classroom communication is no exception. Because much nonverbal behavior is cultural, ITAs should become aware of American classroom norms. For example, *facial expressions convey a speaker's interest in the subject and the audience. In particular, continuous *eye contact is a marvelous tool for enhancing the quality of the communicative act. Gestures are a second component of body language. As a general rule, they should

---

*compound noun

not be conspicuous. Overzealous gestures and a total lack of *hand move-ment are both distracting behaviors. Movement is a third aspect of non-verbal communication. Although standing while speaking is typical for most TAs, some TAs prefer to periodically sit on the desk to create a more informal atmosphere. Furthermore, casual movement around the class-room is considered desirable by most experts; standing completely still signals a lack of confidence. All instructors should become aware of their personal habits and styles in order to take advantage of the enormous power of nonverbal communication.

Reading 2

Since World War II, governmental spending in the United States has in-creased tremendously. The physical sciences, as well as the arts, have received generous support from the government. People who are critical of this governmental intervention generally assert that it will gradually re-sult in too much ideological control of the people. However, others be-lieve that individual *society members, as well as U.S. businesses, can become better educated and more prosperous as a result of technological and artistic developments.

☛ **EXERCISE 3.**   In the sentences below,
a. Identify, analyze, and mark the stress on V/VC Stress Rule words.
b. Read the sentences aloud.
c. Discuss how you would handle each situation.

Sometimes students cause unexpected disruptions in class that require a quick, tactful, and fair response from the instructor. It is important for instructors to be prepared for such situations. Following are some examples.

---

*compound noun

1. A student continually arrives late to class.

2. A student interrupts your lecture with an unusual question.

3. Numerous students refuse to participate in the small group discussions.

4. A student starts vigorously objecting to the way you scored his or her test.

5. Two students continuously talk with each other during your lecture.

6. A student makes a sexually offensive comment during a class discussion.

REVIEW

For words with V/VC endings, the following rule applies.

V/VC Stress Rule			
Part 1:	Keys spelled V or VC	innocuous residual fortuitous inaugural periodically →	Stress left of key	innócuous resídual fortúitous inaúgural periódically
Part 2:	Otherwise,	cuboidal disastrous focal →	Stress key	cuboídal disástrous fócal

☛ **EXERCISE 1.**   General Academic Terms

        a. Write down your general academic terms that are *-al* or *-ous* adjectives or have final *ic* keys.

        b. Mark the stress.

        c. Read each word aloud.

_____ _____ _____

_____ _____ _____

_____ _____ _____

_____ _____ _____

_____ _____ _____

☞ **EXERCISE 2.**   Specific Academic Terms
　　　　　　　　　a. Write down your specific academic terms that are *-al*
　　　　　　　　　　 or *-ous* adjectives or have final *ic* keys.
　　　　　　　　　b. Mark the stress.
　　　　　　　　　c. Read each word aloud.

_____ _____ _____

_____ _____ _____

_____ _____ _____

_____ _____ _____

_____ _____ _____

☞ **EXERCISE 3.**   Write two dialogs and two short passages.
　　　　　　　　　a. In each, use at least one V/VC Stress Rule general aca-
　　　　　　　　　　 demic term or one V/VC Stress Rule specific academic
　　　　　　　　　　 term.
　　　　　　　　　b. Mark the stress of the V/VC Stress Rule words.
　　　　　　　　　c. Read the dialogs and passages aloud.

Examples:

Biology

T:　Let's review some of the wildflowers indígenous to North America. What
　　 do we know about the carrot or parsley family?
S1:　They are usually aromátic herbs.
S2:　But some species are extremely póisonous.
T:　You're both right. Now let's talk about their biológical characterístics.
　　 What about the shape of their flowers?
S3:　I think most of them are biláterally symmétrical.

Education

　　　In terms of adult learning, social-psychológical theory says that envi-
ronméntal factors affect adults more than biológical markers of develop-
ment like growth and maturation.

W-6B. V/VC Rule Endings -V*nt*, -V*nce*, -V*ncy*

PRACTICE

☞ **EXERCISE 1.** a. Identify, analyze, and mark the stress on V/VC Stress Rule words in the phrases below.
b. Use each phrase to make a complete sentence beginning with "Good *language learners develop competence and fluency by . . ."
c. Read each sentence aloud.

1. making intelligent guesses

2. practicing frequently with friends and acquaintances

3. having confidence in their ability to succeed

4. becoming independent by learning to monitor their own speech

5. organizing linguistic information in a relevant way

6. evaluating their own performance after communicating with someone

7. comparing structures and sounds in the new language with those in their dominant language

8. realizing that mistakes are not a sign of ignorance but a natural part of the language learning process

9. trying to understand culturally based differences in behavior

10. using inference, or available contextual and linguistic information, to guess meanings of new words or phrases

11. understanding their dominant *learning style and exploiting their most efficient methods of learning

12. recognizing the redundancy of the language and developing an acceptance that they do not need to understand every single word they read or hear

---

*compound noun

☞ **EXERCISE 2.**   Discussion
Based on the ideas presented in Exercise 1,
a. Choose one statement and give one specific example of a time when you have used this strategy.
b. Choose one strategy that you do not use and discuss whether you could use it in the future.
c. Think of other strategies you use that help you learn English. Discuss them with a partner.

☞ **EXERCISE 3.**   Famous Quotations
a. Identify V/VC Stress Rule words in the quotations below and mark the stress.
b. Read each quote aloud.
c. Choose one quotation and explain what you think it means.

The best argument is that which seems merely an explanation.

—Dale Carnegie

Leaders have a significant role in creating the state of mind that is society.

—John Gardner

The main thing needed to make men happy is intelligence . . . and it can be fostered by education.

—Bertrand Russell

Next in importance to freedom and justice is popular education, without which neither freedom nor justice can be permanently maintained.

—James A. Garfield

REVIEW

For words with V/VC rule endings, the following rule applies.

V/VC Stress Rule			
Part 1:	Keys spelled V or VC	continuant tolerance	→	Stress left of key	contínuant tólerance
Part 2:	Otherwise,	accountancy emergence distance	→	Stress key	accoúntancy emérgence dístance

● **EXERCISE 1.**   General Academic Terms
a. Write down your general academic terms that have *-ant, -ance, -ancy* or *-ent, -ence, -ency* V/VC rule endings.
b. Mark the stress.
c. Read each word aloud.

_____   _____   _____

_____   _____   _____

_____   _____   _____

_____   _____   _____

_____   _____   _____

● **EXERCISE 2.**   Specific Academic Terms
a. Write down your specific academic terms that have *-ant, -ance, -ancy* or *-ent, -ence, -ency* V/VC rule endings.
b. Mark the stress.
c. Read each word aloud.

_____   _____   _____

_____   _____   _____

_____   _____   _____

_____   _____   _____

_____   _____

☛ **EXERCISE 3.**   Write two dialogs and two short passages.
    a. In each, use at least one general academic term or one
       specific academic term with an -*ant, -ance, -ancy* or
       -*ent, -ence, -ency* V/VC rule ending.
    b. Mark the stress of the V/VC Stress Rule words.
    c. Read the dialogs and passages aloud.

Examples:

Geography

A: What is a subsístence economy?
B: In this system, people just produce goods and services for themselves or
       their immediate families. Exchanges in the marketplace are of minor im-
       pórtance.

Physics

       Let's say a conductor is charged with a quantity Q to a potential V. The
       capácitance is $C = Q/V$ ("C equals Q over V").

LEFT STRESS RULE: PRACTICE AND REVIEW

W-7A. Left Rule Endings -*y*/-*i* on Long Words

PRACTICE

☛ **EXERCISE 1.** In the following readings,
a. Identify Left Stress Rule words and mark their stress.
b. Read the passages aloud.

Reading 1

"Umm" and "uhh" are often identified with nervous or incompetent speakers. But in reality, according to the March 1991 *Journal of Personality and Social Psychology,* they are more a function of the speaker's topic. Art and the humanities yield a higher "uhh" rate than chemistry and mathematics.

Two researchers, Stanley Schacter and Nicholas Christenfeld, quantified the "uhhs per minute" (UPM) in the speech of 41 classroom lectures in 10 academic fields. Overall, natural science lecturers registered 1.39 UPM, social science lecturers, 3.84, and humanities lecturers, 4.82. Biology lectures had the lowest UPM rate—less than one "uhh" per minute. English *literature classes were highest at 6.54 UPM.

---

*compound noun

The authors of the article speculated that natural science fields contain more specific terminology, so speakers have fewer choices among words. In the humanities, there is less regularity in descriptions, and thus speakers have more room for creativity.

Adapted from AP article in the *Daily Illini,* University of Illinois, April 19, 1991. Reprinted by permission of the Associated Press.

Reading 2

Since TAs will frequently encounter students from fraternities and sororities, it is important to understand something about them. They are social organizations for undergraduate students. Most fraternities (for men) and sororities (for women) have houses where their members live. Their members are often called "Greeks" because most houses are identified by their Greek letters, such as ΑΤΩ, ΚΑθ, ΔΓ, etc.

The college fraternity movement began in 1776 at the College of William and Mary. It arose from the students' need to belong to some special sort of social community. Early on they were secret societies, and they developed secret oaths, rituals, and *initiation ceremonies, many of which still exist today.

Many students classify Greeks as elitist groups of social snobs. Many TAs stereotype them as superficial, lacking in individuality, and uncommitted to academics. Others view the *Greek system more positively—as an opportunity for new friendships, social activities, and philanthropy for the local community.

---

*compound noun

Regardless of your impressions of Greeks, it is important to realize that membership in sororities and fraternities should have no significant relationship to students' pursuits in the classroom or the quality of their scholarship.

From *College Is Only the Beginning: A Student Guide to Higher Education,* by John N. Gardner and A. Jerome Jewler (Belmont, CA: Wadsworth Publishing Co., 1985), 231–32. ISBN: 0-534-04275-9. Adapted with permission.

☞ **EXERCISE 2.**   Interaction Practice
Part 1. Left Stress Rule Practice

    a. Identify, analyze, and mark the stress on the Left Stress Rule words below.
    b. Read the phrases aloud.

Part 2. React

Rank the items according to your own personal goals and values. That is, put a 1 by the most important goal to you, a 2 by the next most important, etc., through 10.

Part 3. With a Partner

Interview a classmate, and ask him or her to rank the items. Then compare your ratings with each other.

Part 4. Out of Class

Identify and interview an American undergraduate student. Ask him or her to rank the items. Then compare the results with the others.

	Mine	A Classmate's	An Undergrad's
financial security	_____	_____	_____
satisfying personal relationships	_____	_____	_____
opportunity for adventure	_____	_____	_____
stability in a job	_____	_____	_____
a satisfying religion	_____	_____	_____
freedom from anxiety	_____	_____	_____
recognition as an authority in your field	_____	_____	_____
ability to express yourself with clarity	_____	_____	_____
opportunity for creativity	_____	_____	_____
a consistent philosophy of life	_____	_____	_____

REVIEW

Left Stress Rule

For words with left rule endings, stress the left syllable.

☞ **EXERCISE 1.**   General Academic Terms
　　　　　　　　　　　a. Write down your general academic terms that have *-y/-i*
　　　　　　　　　　　　left rule endings.
　　　　　　　　　　　b. Mark the stress.
　　　　　　　　　　　c. Read each word aloud.

_____   _____   _____

_____   _____   _____

_____   _____   _____

_____   _____   _____

_____   _____   _____

☞ **EXERCISE 2.**   Specific Academic Terms
　　　　　　　　　　　a. Write down your specific academic terms that have *-y/-i*
　　　　　　　　　　　　left rule endings.
　　　　　　　　　　　b. Mark the stress.
　　　　　　　　　　　c. Read each word aloud.

_____   _____   _____

_____   _____   _____

_____   _____   _____

_____   _____   _____

_____   _____   _____

☞ **EXERCISE 3.**   Write two dialogs and two short passages.

         a. In each, use at least one Left Stress Rule general academic term and one Left Stress Rule specific academic term.

         b. Mark the stress of the Left Stress Rule words.

         c. Read the dialogs and passages aloud.

Examples:

Economics

      A bilateral monópoly is a situation in the ecónomy where both the buyer and the seller have some monópoly or monópsony power and neither behaves as a price taker.

Biology

   A: What is a pH meter?

   B: It measures the acídity or alkalínity of compounds.

   A: Right. And if the pH value of a compound is seven or higher, what does that sígnify?

   B: It means that it's a base.

W-7B. Left Rule Endings *-ate, -acy*

PRACTICE

☞ **EXERCISE 1.**   a. Identify Left Stress Rule words in the sentences, the dialogs, and the reading below.
        b. Mark the stress on these words.
        c. Read each of the sentences, the dialogs, and the passage aloud.

1. In order to communicate effectively, we have to concentrate on improving our accuracy and our fluency in English.

2. Let's ask our coordinator to identify a qualified candidate—someone who's an expert on literacy.

3. She was devastated by the quality of the class: The professor was overrated, and the lectures were unrelated to the syllabus.

4. After you calculate your results, let's tabulate them and see if they correlate with mine.

5. Our methodology will simplify the experimental design, but unfortunately the results may not approximate reality.

6. Could you comment on the efficacy of the policy?

7. Our purpose is to clarify some of the intricacies of DNA.

Situation 1. Two postdoctoral students talking

   A: Where were you educated?

   B: At the University of Illinois.

   A: As a *graduate student?

   B: Yes. I got my Ph.D. there in kinesiology.

---

*compound noun

Situation 2. A TA and a student discussing homework

A: What are some of the inadequacies of this report?

B: I think some of the assumptions were inaccurate.

Situation 3. Two roommates

A: What is your project for your corporate *policy class?

B: I'm going to do an annotated bibliography of the research on productivity management.

Reading

Goals in Higher Education

Many U.S. universities attempt to integrate teaching, research, and public service. And teaching—in particular, the quality of undergraduate education—has become a priority on many university campuses. Advances in technology and an increased focus on student diversity have made the mission of educating undergraduates rather complicated. But university administrators are beginning to coordinate efforts to respond to the changing society and the changing needs of students today. Their goals are to provide quality instruction to prepare all students for the coming century and to ensure the adequacy and even excellence of our institutions of higher learning.

---

*compound noun

☞ **EXERCISE 2.**   Class Activity

a. Analyze the Left Stress Rule words below.
  • Underline the key and mark the stress.
  • Read each word aloud.
b. Choose two words to complete the sentences below the words.
c. Read your sentences aloud to the class.
d. Take a vote: Does the class agree or disagree with you?

communicate	demonstrate	exaggerate	originate
educate	coordinate	integrate	hesitate
intimidate	concentrate	facilitate	collaborate
articulate	irritate	accommodate	motivate

Complete these sentences.

A good professor should _____.

And a good professor should also _____.

Examples:

A good professor should be motivating.
And a good professor should also try to integrate teaching and research.

REVIEW

> ### Left Stress Rule
>
> For words with left rule endings, stress the left syllable.

☛ **EXERCISE 1.**   General Academic Terms
         a. Identify and write down all of your general academic
            terms that have -*at* + B or -*acy* left rule endings.
         b. Underline the key and mark the stress.
         c. Read each word aloud.

_____   _____   _____

_____   _____   _____

_____   _____   _____

_____   _____   _____

_____   _____   _____

☛ **EXERCISE 2.**   Specific Academic Terms
         a. Identify and write down all of your specific academic
            terms that have -*at* + B or -*acy* left rule endings.
         b. Underline the key and mark the stress.
         c. Read each word aloud.

_____   _____   _____

_____   _____   _____

_____   _____   _____

_____   _____   _____

_____   _____   _____

☞ **EXERCISE 3.**   Write one dialog and one short passage.

a. In each, use at least one Left Stress Rule general academic term or one specific academic term with -*at* + B or -*acy* left rule endings.

b. Mark the stress.

c. Read the dialog and passage aloud.

Examples:

Research Methodology

It is up to the principal invéstigator to ensure that ádequate and ethical procedures are being used in the *research project.

Foreign Languages

A: According to the reading, what is one of the debates in teaching students to commúnicate in a foreign language?

B: It has to do with which goal is more important: áccuracy or fluency.

---

*compound noun

PREFIX STRESS RULE: PRACTICE AND REVIEW

W-8A. Prefixes and Stress

PRACTICE

☛ **EXERCISE 1.**
  a. In words with the key syllable underlined, put a line through any neutral prefix. If all or a part of a regular prefix is in the left syllable, write out the prefix. If there is no prefix in the left syllable, leave the blank empty.
  b. Mark the stress.
  c. Read each phrase aloud.

1. a prov<u>o</u>cative article   _____
   on expos<u>i</u>tory writing   _____

2. a retrosp<u>e</u>ctive report   _____
   a contrad<u>i</u>ctory opinion   _____

3. an impr<u>e</u>ssive description   _____
   of extras<u>e</u>nsory perception _____

4. a Confederate cem<u>e</u>tery   _____
   inconcl<u>u</u>sive documentation _____

5. an imperc<u>e</u>ptive comment _____
   an acc<u>u</u>satory reaction   _____

6. inter<u>a</u>ctive teaching   _____
   coop<u>e</u>rative learning   _____

7. aff<u>ir</u>mative action   _____
   nondiscrim<u>i</u>natory policy _____

8. inc<u>i</u>sive analysis   _____
   of counterintu<u>i</u>tive data   _____

9. an *adv<u>i</u>sory board   _____
   for the obs<u>er</u>vatory   _____

10. a leg<u>i</u>slative session   _____
    on app<u>e</u>llative procedures _____

11. occl<u>u</u>sive cap<u>i</u>llaries   _____
    the cor<u>o</u>nary <u>ar</u>tery   _____

12. in succ<u>e</u>ssive attempts   _____
    of corr<u>e</u>ctive procedures _____

13. a compreh<u>e</u>nsive lecture   _____
    on cogn<u>i</u>tive science   _____

14. an overaggr<u>e</u>ssive student _____
    an eff<u>e</u>ctive reply   _____

*compound noun

15. introspective personality _____   17. a subcontrary proposition _____

supersensitive to others _____   a refutatory example   _____

16. an oppressive atmosphere _____   18. a productive meeting   _____

an abrasive instructor   _____   on communicative goals   _____

☛ **EXERCISE 2.**   Discovering Your Personal Style
Part 1

    a. In the words below, decide whether there is a regular prefix (all or part) in the left syllable.
      • If there is one, write it out.
      • If there is no part of a regular prefix in the left syllable, write the word *none*.
    b. Mark the stress.
    c. Read each word aloud.

Part 2

    a. Rate yourself on each characteristic using the continuum on the rating scale.
      5 = "describes me very well"
      4 = "describes me a little"
      3 = "undecided or neutral"
      2 = "does not describe me too well"
      1 = "does not describe me at all"
    b. Compare the results with your classmates.

Part 3. Discuss the following questions in class.

    a. Do you think any of these characteristics affect the way you learn English? Explain with an example.
    b. Choose one or two characteristics. Describe advantages and disadvantages of having a 5 in this trait.
    c. Why is it important for TAs to be aware of individual differences in students' styles?

**Prefix
in Left?** **Characteristic** **Rating Scale**

	Characteristic					
_____	1. introspective	5	4	3	2	1
_____	2. effective at managing time	5	4	3	2	1
_____	3. likes to put things in categories	5	4	3	2	1
_____	4. intuitive	5	4	3	2	1
_____	5. cognitive	5	4	3	2	1
_____	6. apprehensive about examinations	5	4	3	2	1
_____	7. tentative	5	4	3	2	1
_____	8. affective	5	4	3	2	1
_____	9. subjective	5	4	3	2	1
_____	10. imaginative	5	4	3	2	1
_____	11. perceptive	5	4	3	2	1
_____	12. attentive to detail	5	4	3	2	1
_____	13. great expenditure of energy	5	4	3	2	1
_____	14. assertive	5	4	3	2	1
_____	15. intensive	5	4	3	2	1
_____	16. speculative	5	4	3	2	1

REVIEW

Summary: Prefixes

Learn to recognize the following prefixes in words.

Neutral: *counter-/contra-, inter-/intro-, extra-, over-, retro-, super-*

Regular: *de-, re-, pre-, pro-, per-, ad-, ab-, ob-, sub-, in-, con-, com-, ex-, dis-*

Remember, *in-* is a prefix only when it begins a word or when it is after a neutral prefix.

Alternate Forms

ac + c	af + f	ag + g	al + l	ap + p	at + t	as + s
oc + c	of + f	op + p	col + l	cor + r		
dif + f	ef + f	il + l	im + p	suc + c		

For words with prefix rule endings, the following rule applies.

Prefix Stress Rule

When no part of a prefix is in the left syllable, stress left. If you can't stress left, stress the key.

~~inter~~áctive	~~extra~~sénsory	refínery	apprehénsive	unprovócative
inquísitive	cátegory	mónastery	appósitive	spéculative

☞ **EXERCISE**   a. Draw a wavy line (〜) under the left syllable of the words below.
b. Draw a line (———) through any neutral prefixes.
c. Mark the stress.
d. Answer the questions that follow.
e. Read each word aloud.

assimilative	superaggressive	secondary	recriminatory
profanatory	comparative	coronary	repetitive
musculature	administrative	counterproductive	chancellery
appellative	predictive	compulsory	itinerary
refectory	caricature	distillery	contemporary

1. Neutral prefixes
   Find examples of neutral prefixes.

   _____

   How should neutral prefixes be treated when analyzing words?

   _____

2. Regular prefixes
   Find examples of these three possible types of left syllables.
   Write down all of the words.

   No part of a regular prefix is in the left syllable, as in *literary*.

   _____

   _____

   The whole regular prefix is in the left syllable, as in *affective*.

   _____

   _____

   Only a **part** of the regular prefix is in the left syllable—only its last letter, or last two letters, as in *protective* and *collective*.

   _____

   _____

3. What part of a regular prefix must be in the left syllable to count as a "prefix part in the left syllable"?

_____

4. When is *in-* **not** considered a regular prefix?

_____

Find examples in the list above of *in-* in this situation.

_____

W-8B. Prefix Rule Endings
-ary, -ery, -ory, -ive

PRACTICE

☞ **EXERCISE 1.**   Dialogs
a. Identify Prefix Stress Rule words in each dialog below.
b. Mark the major stress.
c. Read each dialog aloud with a partner.

Situation 1. Two graduate students in the College of Education

A: Did you get a *teaching assistantship for fall? I just found out I'm teaching either History of Secondary Education or Perspectives in Child Psychology.

B: I haven't heard anything yet. I suppose I'll still be teaching Art for *Elementary Teachers. Since I've been teaching it for two years, I'm hoping the professor will give me some supervisory responsibilities.

Situation 2. Two roommates talking

A: I can't believe I'm voluntarily taking this public *speaking class.

B: Why? I remember you saying that the TA was extraordinary.

A: Extraordinarily demanding is more like it. Today was our fourth extemporary speech.

B: Really? What did you talk about?

A: Some recent discoveries about what happens to the arteries during coronary attacks.

B: Why didn't you talk about something easier, like life in the student dormitories?

---

*compound noun

Situation 3. Two political science TAs

A: Did you hear about that documentary on Hungary? It certainly wasn't objective!

B: I know. The top *military official is supposed to give a commentary tonight on the news. I think I'll have my students watch it as a *homework assignment.

Situation 4. Two TAs talking

A: I'm having a problem. One of my students has missed a lot of class. His grades are pretty impressive, but attendance is compulsory, so I don't know what to do.

B: Why don't you talk to the TA *advisory committee? They might be able to tell you about the department's policies.

☛ **EXERCISE 2.**   Prefix Stress Rule Adjectives and Nouns
a. Mark the major stress in each Prefix Stress Rule adjective and noun below.
b. Read each word aloud.
c. Then choose an adjective or a noun to complete each of the numbered sentences.
d. Read each sentence aloud.

Adjectives

distinctive	sanitary	imaginary	compulsory
cognitive	momentary	extemporary	contradictory

1. It's something you have to do. It's _____.

2. It's unplanned or spontaneous, like a speech. It's _____.

3. It's unique, not like the others. It's _____.

4. It's very clean. It's _____.

---

*compound noun

5. It's done with the brain. It's _____.

6. It's only for a short time. It's _____.

7. It's a statement saying the opposite of another statement. It's _____.

8. It's something you dreamed or invented. It's _____.

Nouns

objective	itinerary	monastery	category
fugitive	obituary	refinery	dormitory

1. It's a *residence hall. It's a(n) _____.

2. It's running away from something. It's a(n) _____.

3. It's a plan for a trip or journey. It's a(n) _____.

4. It's a kind of factory, as for making gasoline. It's a(n) _____.

5. It's an article about someone who has just died. It's a(n) _____.

6. It'a goal, or something you work toward. It's a(n) _____.

7. It's a class of things, or a classification. It's a(n) _____.

8. It's a place where monks live and work. It's a(n) _____.

☛ **EXERCISE 3.**   Prefix Stress Rule Words in Context
a. Mark the major stress in each Prefix Stress Rule word below.
b. Read each word aloud.
c. Suppose it is the first day of class and you are introducing the course and yourself to your students. Prepare a three-minute introduction using the phrases below.
d. Practice your introduction with a classmate.

History 252
History of Scientific Discoveries

Prerequisite: An introductory course in physics.

Class meetings: Mondays and Wednesdays in room 45, Cognitive Sciences Building

---

*compound noun

Requirements:	Three short essays
	Interactive participation in class discussions (attendance is compulsory!)
	One library research paper
Textbook:	*Historical Perspectives on Science,* by Robert T. Crane (1993)
	Also required is a packet of supplementary readings, available for $6.50 from the departmental secretary.
Instructor:	(Say something about yourself!)

REVIEW

For words with prefix rule endings, the following rule applies.

Prefix Stress Rule

When no part of a prefix is in the left syllable, stress left. If you can't stress left, stress the key.

☞ **EXERCISE 1.**   General Academic Terms
  a. Write down your general academic terms that have *-ary, -ory, -ery,* and *-ive* prefix rule endings.
  b. Mark the stress.
  c. Read each word aloud.

_____	_____	_____
_____	_____	_____
_____	_____	_____
_____	_____	_____
_____	_____	_____

☞ **EXERCISE 2.**   Specific Academic Terms
  a. Write down your specific academic terms that have *-ary, -ory, -ery,* and *-ive* prefix rule endings.
  b. Mark the stress.
  c. Read each word aloud.

_____	_____	_____
_____	_____	_____
_____	_____	_____
_____	_____	_____
_____	_____	_____

☞ **EXERCISE 3.**   Write two dialogs and two short passages.

a. In each, use at least one Prefix Stress Rule general academic term or one Prefix Stress Rule specific academic term.

b. Mark the stress of the Prefix Stress Rule words.

c. Read the dialogs and passages aloud.

Examples:

Economics

A: What is the International Mónetary Fund?

B: It's an organization of the United Nations. Its prímary function is to coordinate international payments and trade.

Geography

The discóvery of Machu Picchu was led by Hiram Bingham, an American archaeologist who wrote a careful description of it in his díary. One of the most intriguing parts of Machu Picchu is an impréssive sánctuary.

W-8C. Prefix Rule Endings
-ative, -atory, -ature

PRACTICE

☛ **EXERCISE 1.**   a. Identify Prefix Stress Rule words in each phrase.
b. Mark the stress.
c. Read each pair of phrases aloud.
d. Choose one of the pairs and explain to a partner what it means.

The Dissertation

1. exploratory *research questions

   provocative ideas

2. authoritative references

   *literature review

3. speculative hypotheses

   educative value

4. investigative procedures

   qualitative or quantitative?

5. explanatory discussion of results

   representative of reality?

6. the editing: conservative revisions

   the defense: recapitulative of your work

7. your adviser's signature

   a commemorative symbol

---

*compound noun

☞ **EXERCISE 2.**   a. Identify Prefix Stress Rule words in each column.
b. Mark the major stress.
c. Match a course in column A with the appropriate building in column B by drawing a line between them.
d. For each matched pair, complete the following sentence aloud.

"_____ meets in (the) _____."
       (course)   (building)

Column A
Courses

Perspectives in Astronomy

Administrative Leadership in Education

Studies in Comparative Cinema

Communicative Approaches to Language

   Teaching

Contemporary Orchestral Literature

Quantitative Genetics

Historical Perspectives in Judicature

Column B
Buildings

Biological Sciences Laboratory

Foreign Languages Building

the Music Conservatory

the Law Library

Arts and Literature Building

the Observatory

Education Building

☞ **EXERCISE 3.**   a. Select one of the courses in Exercise 2.
b. Explain to a partner why you would like to take that course (or why not).

REVIEW

For words with prefix rule endings, the following rule applies.

Prefix Stress Rule

When no part of a prefix is in the left syllable, stress left. If you can't stress left, stress the key.

☞ **EXERCISE 1.**   General Academic Terms
a. Write down your general academic terms that have *-ative, -atory,* and *-ature* prefix rule endings.
b. Mark the stress.
c. Read each word aloud.

_____   _____   _____

_____   _____   _____

_____   _____   _____

_____   _____   _____

_____   _____   _____

☞ **EXERCISE 2.**   Specific Academic Terms
a. Write down your specific academic terms that have *-ative, -atory,* and *-ature* prefix rule endings.
b. Mark the stress.
c. Read each word aloud.

_____   _____   _____

_____   _____   _____

_____   _____   _____

_____   _____   _____

_____   _____   _____

☞ **EXERCISE 3.**   Write two short homework assignments and two short test questions.

     a. In each, use at least one Prefix Stress Rule general academic term or one Prefix Stress Rule specific academic term.

     b. Mark the stress of the Prefix Stress Rule words.

     c. Read the assignments and questions aloud.

Examples:

Biology

     Your next assignment is to begin learning the nómenclature of the local *wildflowers.

Speech Communications

     What are the elements of a declámatory rhetorical style?

---

*compound noun

W-9

STRESS OF CONSTRUCTIONS

W-9A. Compound Nouns 1

☞ **EXERCISE 1.** Listen to each phrase and circle the word that receives more stress.

Example: (reference) desk

1. biology test
2. horizontal axis
3. literature review
4. easy assignments

5. independent variable
6. sample size
7. fair grades
8. grammar rules

The items where you circled the second word are Adjective + Noun. The items where you circled the first word are **compound nouns.** Compound nouns are special pairs of words that have some distinct meaning together. They function as a single vocabulary word.

Noun + Noun

Usually compound nouns consist of pairs of nouns. Some familiar examples are

research paper	time limit	lab equipment
homework	problem set	textbook
page number	book review	database

Also, (course subject) + "class/course/lab"

my math class
the new chemistry course
her physics lab

Most compound nouns have a special stress and intonation. You will be much more intelligible if you use the right rhythm and melody for compounds.

In most compound nouns, the first word in each pair (marked ○) gets more stress and a higher pitch. The second word (marked ˋ) gets less stress; it is spoken at a lower pitch.

○
research pàper

☛ **EXERCISE 2.**   Repeat the phrases above using compound noun stress and intonation. Remember to use a higher pitch on the first word and a lower pitch on the second word.

The stress of compound nouns is different from adjective-noun stress. Earlier you learned that primary phrase stress falls on the last content word in new information. In Adjective + Noun cases, this holds true. Compare the following.

Adjective + Noun

        ○
a scientìfic discovery
hypothetical cases
a detailed graph
a controversial statement

Compound Noun

  ○
a science pròject
hypothesis testing
a bar graph
a thesis statement

Question: What is the difference between

      ○
a Spànish teacher   and

     ○
a Spanish teàcher?

☛ **EXERCISE 3.**   a. In the following dialogs, underline compound nouns.
b. Mark the stress on the compound nouns with ○.
c. Read the dialogs aloud.

Situation 1. Grad student and professor

G: I want to apply to be a lab assistant.

P: Well, first you'll have to take the SPEAK test.

G: What's that?

P: It's an oral proficiency test. You speak into a tape recorder. I believe they're giving one next month.

G: OK. How can I study for it?

P: There's a practice test in the ESL Listening Lab.

Situation 2. Two new TAs

A: How can you get into the computer lab?

B: You need your identification card.

Situation 3. Two grad students

A: When did you enter the graduate program?

B: Last semester.

A: Do you like it?

B: Yes, I do. The course work has been really good. And I'm going to talk to the department head about being her research assistant, so I can get some experience, too.

Situation 4. Two TAs in their office

A: What are you doing?

B: I'm writing a new computer program. It is going to help me keep track of my students' test scores.

A: That sounds good. A computer is great for record keeping, isn't it?

B: Yeah. It's great for data analysis, too. I'm hoping it will help me compare the scores of my two discussion sections.

Situation 5. Two students in the same class

A: I missed history class on Friday. Do you have the lecture notes?

B: Sure. They announced a review session for the next test.

A: What test?

B: An essay test on the Iron Age. It's on Monday.

A: Well, I guess I'll have to study all weekend.

Situation 6. Roommates

A: I'm going to the bookstore. I need to get some computer paper and a textbook for my rhetoric class. Do you want to go?

B: I'd better not. I have to finish my lab report. But could you pick up a spiral
notebook for me?

A: Sure, no problem. You can pay me when I get back.

> NOTE: Compound noun stress works with Noun + Noun combinations 90
> percent of the time. Much of the other 10 percent consists of special cate-
> gories of words that will be addressed in the next units. Otherwise, you
> will nearly always be correct if you stress the first element of compound
> noun combinations. Virtually all of the hyphenated compound nouns, as
> well as those written as one word, are stressed on the first element.

☞ **EXERCISE 4.**   a. Mark the stress on the compound nouns below with ○ ˋ.
  b. Read them aloud.
  c. Ask a partner for some information about each one. For
     example, "Who's your office mate?"

office mate	thesis committee	discussion section
English class	dissertation topic	homework
science lab	data analysis	culture shock
art studio	phone number	department head

Other Types of Compound Nouns

Adjective + Noun as compound noun

   Adjective + Noun combinations sometimes form a single noun and are stressed
on the first word. Often, some special meaning is attached.

Examples:

A **whìte house** refers to any home that is white in color, but the **White Hoùse**
   is where the president of the United States lives.

A **hòt plate** is a dish that is very warm, but a **hot plàte** is an appliance for
   cooking.

On the surface, these terms look virtually the same. Therefore it is difficult to predict whether such phrases are compound nouns or not, especially without knowing the meaning. However, when you hear others use compound noun stress on such terms, it is important to recognize them as a single noun. Try using your ears to identify all kinds of compound nouns—they are everywhere in speech!

Some other examples of compound nouns beginning with an adjective:

social life	blackboard	darkroom
software	high school	sweetheart
nervous system	cold front	greenhouse

> REMINDER: When adjectives are in the first position, check to see if the term is hyphenated or written as a single word—these are excellent signals for compound noun stress.

There are also many *-ing* + Noun combinations that form compound nouns.

teaching assistant	dining hall	parking lot
reading room	qualifying exam	magnifying glass
turning point	learning disorder	writing style

Notice that the *-ing* word does not so much describe the following noun but combines with it to name something special. In such cases, compound noun stress is prevalent.

☞ **EXERCISE 5.**   Read the above phrases aloud.

Sometimes compound nouns consist of more than two words. In general, the stress goes on the second-to-last word.

○

Examples: an educàtion reform mòvement

the Consumer Price Index	the office copy machine
a staff development seminar	a business database
the human motor cortex	stimulus response theory

However, sometimes a noun is added after an already existing compound noun pair. In these cases, the first word of the original pair is stressed.

○

Examples: **learning style** prèferences

your **English class** assignment   our **term paper** deadline
a **letter writing** campaign   some **thesis committee** problems
my **math test** grade   a **lesson plan** format

☞ **EXERCISE 6.**   Read the above phrases aloud.

☞ **EXERCISE 7.**   Computer Terms
                       a. With a partner, identify a compound noun that fits each
                          description below.
                       b. Monitor your use of compound stress.

1. Where you move or use the mouse
2. What you type on
3. A program that displays a graphic design to protect the screen
4. Your working environment on the computer (the menu bar and the background area on the screen)
5. This program organizes the internal activities of the computer, such as managing information in memory
6. This is a unique set of characters that a network user must type in before accessing a computer or an e-mail account

☛ **EXERCISE 8.**   Write down fifteen compound nouns from your field of study. Choose compound nouns that you use frequently. You will be responsible for pronouncing them correctly. So practice them!

	COMPOUND NOUNS	ADJECTIVE-NOUNS (Compare: *Not* compound noun stress)
ECONOMICS	budget line, demand curve, price index	dual economy
BIOLOGY	frame shift, memory cell, plasma membrane	induced enzyme
EDUCATION	intelligence quotient, learning curve, stimulus-response theory	cognitive learning
STATISTICS	halo effect, correlation coefficient, regression analysis	random sample
GEOLOGY	contour map, greenhouse effect, meteor shower	continental drift

My Compound Nouns

_____   _____   _____

_____   _____   _____

_____   _____   _____

_____   _____   _____

_____   _____   _____

☞ **EXERCISE 9.**   a. Write fifteen meaningful sentences, each containing one of your compound nouns.

b. Read each sentence aloud.

☞ **EXERCISE 10.**   a. Choose one of the compound nouns you selected.

b. Give a brief definition of it to a partner.

☞ **EXERCISE 11.**   a. Audiotape (with permission) a professor teaching a class in your field of study.

b. Write down all the compound nouns you hear.

c. Say the compound nouns aloud several times.

W-9B. Compound Nouns 2

Some noun combinations do *not* follow compound noun stress. The following sets of words are important examples.

Names of People

◯

Stress the last word. For example, "Albert Einstein."

Mary Kay
Mary Kay Bender
Professor Bender
Professor Mary Kay Bender

Stanley Foster
President Foster
President Stanley Foster

Michael Talbot
Dean Talbot
Dean Michael Talbot

Kathryn Martin
Chancellor Martin
Chancellor Kathryn Martin

☛ **EXERCISE 1.**   a. Put ◯ on the correct part of the names in the following dialog. The first one is done for you.
b. Practice the dialog aloud with a partner.

A: Who's your math professor?

◯
B: Professor Tom Spencer.

A: Is Richard Hart still there?

B: Yes, but Dr. Gonzales is doing most of his work.

A: Isn't she in charge of the tutoring program, too?

B: No, Michael Goldstein is.

NOTE: Many graduate students (American and international alike) are concerned about how to address their professors. That is, some professors prefer to be called "Dr. Spencer" or "Professor Spencer," while others prefer to be called by their first names, for example, "Tom." In many cases this depends on the individual professor, and in some cases it depends on the "culture" or protocol of the department. Many graduate students who are in doubt begin with the more formal "Dr. Spencer" and wait for the professor to offer, "You can call me Tom." It is also a good idea to check with other graduate students to find out what different professors prefer. Nearly all TAs and undergraduate students, however, are on a first-name basis with each other.

☛ **EXERCISE 2.**   Supply the following information.

Who is the dean of your college?   _____

Who is the head of your department?   _____

Who is your adviser?   _____

Who is an American TA in your department?   _____

Publications

○

Stress the last word. For example, "the *Daily Planet*."

the *L.A. Times*   *Psychology Today*
the *Chicago Tribune*   *U.S. News and World Report*
the *Wall Street Journal*   the *Chronicle of Higher Education*

☛ **EXERCISE 3.**   a. Write down the titles of the three most important journals in your field.
                     b. Read them aloud.

1. _____

2. _____

3. _____

☛ **EXERCISE 4.**   Practice the following dialog.

A: I've looked through the *New York Times* and the *Washington Post,* but I can't find any recent articles on my research topic.

B: Why don't you try some business magazines, such as *Investors Weekly* and *Crain's Chicago Business*?

Abbreviations

○
Stress the last letter. For example, "E S L."

CBS	SAT	IBM	ITA	UCLA
NBC	ACT	CPU	TSE	BYU
ABC	GRE	PC	GPA	FSU

☞ **EXERCISE 5.**   a. Write down three of the most common abbreviations in your field.
b. Read them aloud.

1. _____   2. _____   3. _____

Chemical Compounds

○
Stress the last word. For example, "carbon dioxide."

propyl ether   hydrogen chloride
nickel carbonyl   sodium hydrogen sulfate
nitrogen dioxide   ethyl benzene

Others:

_____   _____

_____   _____

_____   _____

_____   _____

Noun 2 Is Made out of Noun 1

When the first noun tells the material out of which the second noun is made, the second noun usually receives more stress.

Example: a stone wall

steel container
plastic bag
hydrogen ions
copper wire

brick building
paper airplane
acid rain
glass beaker

Others:

_____   _____

_____   _____

_____   _____

_____   _____

Time + Noun

When the first noun indicates the time when the second noun takes place or is scheduled, the second noun usually receives more stress.

Example: the evening paper

a noon appointment
spring break
fall semester

the morning news
the summer timetable
my 10:00 class

Others:

_____   _____

_____   _____

_____   _____

_____   _____

☞ **EXERCISE 6.**   a. Complete the following dialog with your own information.
                    b. Read the dialog aloud with a partner.

Situation. Looking for a journal

A: Excuse me, Professor _____ (name of your adviser).

B: Hi, _____ (your name). What's up?

A: I'm looking for the most recent issue of _____
      (journal in your field). Do you have a copy I could borrow?

B: Yes, I do. But I think it's at home. I could bring it in tomorrow for you.

A: That would be great. Let's see. . . . I have a _____ (time) o'clock
      class. Could I pick it up after that?

B: Sure. No problem.

☞ **EXERCISE 7.**   a. Choose one term from each category below.
                    b. Write three short dialogs. Each dialog should contain
                       one of the terms you selected.
                    c. Put ◯ on the correct part of the term.
                    d. Read the dialogs aloud with a partner.

Initials	Noun 2 Made out of Noun 1	Time + Noun
GRE	paper bag	noon seminar
ESL	diamond ring	summer vacation
UCLA	chicken soup	afternoon class

Example:

                                    ◯
A: Did you take the GRE?

B: Yes, I did. But I don't remember my scores.

W-9C. Compound Place-Names

Cities, States, and Countries

Stress the last word.

Examples:

◯	◯	◯
Saint Louis	Urbana, Illinois	Santiago, Chile

☛ **EXERCISE 1.**   Read the following aloud.

City	**City + State**	**City + Country**
New York City	New York, New York	Seoul, Korea
Salt Lake City	Salt Lake City, Utah	São Paulo, Brazil
Ann Arbor	Ann Arbor, Michigan	Paris, France

☛ **EXERCISE 2.**   a. Complete the following dialogs.
                      b. Mark the stress of the places with ◯.
                      c. Read the dialogs aloud with a partner.

A: Where are you from?

B: I'm from _____ (City + Country).

       Where are you from?

A: I'm from _____ (City + Country).

A: What places have you visited in the United States?

B: I've been to _____ (Cities + States). How about you?

A: I've been to _____ (Cities + States).

Universities and Colleges

Stress the last word.

Example:

◯   ◯   ◯

the University of Illinois   Parkland Community College   Iowa State University

☛ **EXERCISE 3.**   Read the following aloud.

the University of Chicago	Northwestern University	Rutgers University
Harvard University	the University of Wyoming	Harper College
Northern Michigan University	DeAnza Community College	Boston University

☛ **EXERCISE 4.**   a. Write down the names of four universities or colleges you are familiar with. Use the answer blanks below.
b. On another piece of paper, write short dialogs using these names.
c. Use ◯ to mark the stress on the college/university names.
d. Read the dialogs aloud with a partner.

1. _____

2. _____

3. _____

4. _____

Streets

◯
1. _____ Street

If it is called a *street*, stress the word preceding "Street."

Main Street	John Street	Second Street
Green Street	East Daniel Street	Thirty-third Street

                ◯
2. _____ Avenue
                  Boulevard
                  Road
                  Way
                  Circle
                  Court, etc.

If it is *not* called a street, stress the last element.

Lincoln Avenue	Meadowbrook Court	Florida Avenue
Williams Boulevard	Smith Road	Persimmon Circle
John Drive	Evergreen Lane	Deerpark Court

☞ **EXERCISE 5.**   Answer the following questions.

1. What street do you live on? _____.

2. What street is your departmental office on? _____.

3. Write down the names of other streets/roads/etc. that you frequently use. Mark the stress with ◯ and read them aloud.

    _____   _____

    _____   _____

    _____   _____

Buildings

Building stress is much less straightforward. Here are some general guidelines; they may not work in all situations.

                                ◯
1. _____ (proper name) + _____ (any building word)

Talbot Lab	Kenney Gym
Roger Adams Lab	Thomas Paine School
Carle Clinic	Coe Library
Davenport Hall	Foellinger Auditorium

But if "the" is included, the stress often seems to be on the proper noun.

     ○   ○

the Beckman Institute   *the* Swanlund Building

     ○

2. _____ (not a proper name) + Building/Lab/Museum/Library/
Clinic/just about everything else

For most other building names, stress the next-to-last word.

Administration Building	Student Services Building
the Psychology Building	Foreign Languages Building
Krannert Art Museum	Natural History Museum
Microelectronics Lab	Materials Research Lab
Forest Science Lab	Aeronautical Engineering Lab
the Law Library	the Education Library
the Ice Arena	Small Animal Clinic
the Fine Arts Center	the Arts and Sciences Auditorium

3. _____ Hall

                                 ○

a. When there are just two words, stress "Hall."

Harker Hall	Commerce Hall	Hoyt Hall
Engineering Hall	Agronomy Hall	Mumford Hall

               ○

b. But note: "*the* _____ Hall."

the Assembly Hall   *the* Statistics Hall

                                               ○

c. And when there are more than two words: "_____ _____
Hall"

Smith Music Hall   Illinois Street Residence Hall

☞ **EXERCISE 6.**   a. Write down the names of six of the buildings you most
frequently enter on campus.
b. Mark the stress.
c. Read each name aloud.

_____   _____

_____   _____

_____   _____

☞ **EXERCISE 7.**   a. Choose two buildings on your campus.
b. Explain to a partner how to get from one to the other.
Use street names and building names.

Example: To get from Digital Computer Lab to Altgeld Hall

Go west on Springfield Avenue until you get to Wright Street. Then go
south on Wright Street. You will pass Talbot Lab on your left. Go across
Green Street. Altgeld Hall is on the southeast corner.

W-9D. Compound Numbers

Compound Numbers Alone

Compound numbers are numbers that consist of two or more parts. Each part consists of one word, either a number or "teen." Compound numbers are written either as hyphenated words (as in "twenty-four") or as one word (with "teen").

Compound numbers are very common in speech. In many cases, we tend to favor making a compound out of a pair of digits ("twenty-four" for 24) or out of the last pair in a larger number ("three twenty-four" for 324).

When no noun follows a compound number, the heaviest stress goes on the last part of the compound.

○	○	○
sìxteen	twènty-four	one hundred thìrty-eight
○	○	○
nìneteen	sìxty-three	two thousand fifty-two

☛ **EXERCISE 1.**
a. Mark the stress on the compound numbers below.
b. Read each course name and number aloud.
c. Write down the names of some classes you are taking or teaching that have compound course numbers.
d. Read each of your own course names and numbers aloud.

Courses

ESL 115   Math 445   Physiology 337   Theater 324   Sociology 413

Your courses

_____	_____
_____	_____
_____	_____
_____	_____

☞ **EXERCISE 2.**　a. Mark the stress on each compound number below with
  ` ○. The first one is done for you.
  b. Read each compound number aloud.
  c. For this set of numbers, find the mean (the average)
  with a partner. Monitor your use of stress on numbers.
  Write down your answer.
  d. Mark the stress on the mean and read it aloud.

` ○
24　19　23　34　13　24　17　23　26　24　33　16

Compound Numbers in Discourse

For this section, it may be helpful to consult Discourse Foundations D-5 in your
core textbook.

Consider the word *sixteen* in these two example dialogs.

Example 1:

　　　　　　　　　○　　●　　　　　●
A:　If Luke was **sixteen** in 1983, | how old is he now?
B:　Twenty-seven.

Example 2:

A:　How old was Luke in 1983?
　　　　　　　●
B:　He was **sixteen.**

In Example 1, "sixteen" is stressed on "teen" because "teen" is the second part
of the compound number that has no following noun.

Sometimes, a compound number falls in a position to receive primary stress. If
it has no following noun, the second part of the compound number receives heavier stress. In Example 2, "sixteen," a compound number, is the last content word
in new information. And "teen" is stressed because it is the second part of the
compound.

☞ **EXERCISE 3.**   Compound Numbers in Discourse
                     a. Mark the stress on each compound number with ◯. If
                        the compound number falls in primary stress position,
                        fill in the circle: ●.
                     b. Read each dialog aloud with a partner.

Example: A math class

                               ◯
   A: What is 47 x 2 (forty-seven times two)?

                           ●
   B: It's 54 (fifty-four).

                                   ◯
   A: Right. And what is 47 x 3 (forty-seven times three)?

                               ●
   B: 141 (one hundred forty-one).

Situation 1. Two students talking

   A: I got a 17 (seventeen) on the quiz.

   B: Out of how many?

   A: Twenty-two.

Situation 2. Two TAs preparing a test

   A: We are supposed to get this test copied for the students. How many do we
          need? About 125 (one twenty-five)?

   B: Well, let's see. I have two sections, | with 19 (nineteen) in each, | and An-
          gela said she has 47 (forty-seven) total.

   A: And I have 31 (thirty-one). So let's just make 116 (one sixteen).

Situation 3. Two colleagues

A: Are you free on October 17th for a meeting?

B: Not really. But I could make it on the 21st (twenty-first).

A: That's fine. Is 2:45 (two forty-five) ok?

B: Yes, it is.

Compound Numbers + Noun

When a compound number modifies a noun, the stress of the compound number shifts from the last part to the second-to-last part.

| ○   ○ | ○   ○ | ○   ○ |
| fifteen pages | twenty-four subjects | one hundred thirty-eight points |

| ○   ○ | ○   ○ | ○   ○ |
| nineteen dollars | sixty-three percent | two thousand fifty-two miles |

☛ **EXERCISE 4.**   a. Mark the stress on each compound number + Noun with ○ ˋ ○.
b. Read each phrase aloud with a partner.

fourteen cents	forty-six students	six hundred fifty-three acres
thirteen chapters	seventy-five types	nine hundred and ninety-nine days
nineteen grams	ninety-four years	four hundred fifty-six pounds

Compound Numbers + Noun in Discourse

Consider the stress of "ninety-three" in the following three example dialogs.

Example 1:

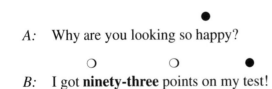

●

A: Why are you looking so happy?

        ○   ○   ●

B: I got **ninety-three** points on my test!

Example 2:

> ●
A: How did you do on your test?

> ○   ●
B: I got **ninety-three** points!

Example 3:

> ●
A: How many points did you get on your test?

> ●
B: I got **ninety-three** points.

In Example 1, "ninety-three" is stressed on "ninety" because "ninety" is the first part of a compound number followed by a noun. "Points," another content word, receives about the same amount of stress as "ninety."

Sometimes, the noun following a compound number falls in a position to receive primary stress. In these cases, the first part of the compound number still receives stress, although less than the following noun. In Example 2, "points," a noun, is the last content word in new information. Therefore it will receive primary stress—heavier than "ninety."

However, in Example 3, the noun ("points") is old information. In such cases, the compound number is stressed as if there were no following noun at all—on the second part of the compound.

☞ **EXERCISE 5.**   a. Mark the primary stress of each message unit with ●.
    b. Mark the stress on each remaining compound number with ○.
    c. Read each dialog aloud with a partner.

Example: In a lab

> ○   ○   ●
A: You will have thirteen days to finish your *lab write-up.

> ●
B: How many pages should it be?

---

*compound noun

         ●   ●

A: As many as it takes. It usually takes at least twenty-five pages, | but you

                   ●

     might be able to do it in less.

                    ●

B: How much of our grade is this worth?

            ○   ●

A: It's worth 35 (thirty-five) percent.

Situation 1. A student setting up a meeting with a TA

A: Do you have about fifteen minutes after class?

B: Sure. But I have a meeting at 4:45 (four forty-five). What did you want to

     talk about?

A: The *homework problem about the thirty-two workers digging sixteen ditches.

B: Fine. That shouldn't take too long.

Situation 2. Two TAs talking

A: On the last test, | how many students got more than 75 (seventy-five) per-

     cent correct?

B: I counted fourteen students.

Situation 3. Running an experiment

A: What's your *sample size for the *control group?

B: One hundred twenty-five subjects.

A: And in the *experimental group?

B: I have one hundred thirty-two subjects.

---

*compound noun

Situation 4. A math problem

A: If it takes Brad 16 (sixteen) hours to go 224 (two hundred twenty-four)

   miles, | what is his rate?

B: 14 (fourteen) miles per hour.

A: Right. And what if it takes him 32 (thirty-two) hours?

B: Then it would be 7 (seven) miles per hour.

☛ **EXERCISE 6.**   a. Mark the stress on each compound number on the left
      with ˋO.
   b. Read each compound number aloud.
   c. With a partner, match each compound number to a
      noun phrase on the right by drawing a line between
      them. Make a complete sentence beginning with
      "There are . . ."
   d. Mark the stress on each new compound number +
      Noun with O ˋ O.
   e. Mark the primary stress with ●.
   f. Read each phrase aloud.

Compound Number	Noun Phrase
twenty-five	days in a year
thirty-six	letters in the Roman alphabet
thirteen	*heart cards in a deck of *playing cards
three hundred sixty-five	ounces in a pound
twenty-four	inches in a yard
fourteen	cents in a U.S. quarter
fifty-two	carats of gold
thirty-one	hours in a day
sixteen	days in January
twenty-six	weeks in a year

*compound noun

☛ **EXERCISE 7.**   a. Complete the following dialogs with a partner.
b. Mark the stress on each compound number + Noun with ○ ˋ ○.
c. If there is no following noun, mark the stress on the compound number with ˋ○.
d. Read each dialog aloud with your partner.

Dialog 1

A: How far is it from _____ to _____?
                                    (place)   (place)

B: It's about _____ miles/blocks/meters/etc.

Dialog 2

A: How long does it take to get to _____?
                                              (place)

B: It takes about _____ minutes/hours/days/etc.

A: And how long does it take to get to _____?
                                                (another place)

B: It takes about _____ minutes/hours/days/etc.

Dialog 3

A: How much does a bicycle cost in your country?

B: It costs about _____ _____.
                            (amount)   (currency)

A: And how much does a television cost in your country?

B: It costs about _____ _____.
                            (amount)   (currency)

Numbers in Contrast

☞ **EXERCISE 8.**   a. Listen to the following dialog.
b. For each compound number, circle the part that receives more stress.

Situation. Two TAs grading exams

A: Oh, no. I just realized that I miscalculated one of my students' *test scores.

He should have gotten an 87 (eighty-seven), | not a 77 (seventy-seven).

B: You should go tell Professor Chen. Do you know where to find her?

A: I think she's in either room 124 (one twenty-four) | or 134 (one thirty-four). I'll go check.

When we talk about numbers, we are often contrasting their parts. In these cases, the stress of compound numbers may change from the expected rhythms we have already looked at. That is because when we make contrasts, we place primary stress on the particular word(s) or word part(s) that are in contrast.

The section Discourse Domains D-8: Comparing and Contrasting describes six types of contrasts. Study the primary stress of compound numbers in the following examples.

Example 1:   Choice questions

A: I couldn't hear what you said. Is it 288 (two hundred eighty-eight) miles |

or 289 (two hundred eighty-nine) miles?

B: Two hundred eighty-nine miles.

Example 2:   *Either . . . or*

A: The Great Wall of China was built as a *defense system under the first emperor.
B: When was it completed?

A: I'm not really sure. It was either 214 (two fourteen) B.C., | or 216 (two sixteen) B.C. I'll have to check and let you know.

---

*compound noun

Example 3:   Comparative

                    ●   ●

The *pie graph on page thirteen is clearer than the one on page sixteen.

Example 4:   [not *x*, but *y*]; [*x*, not *y*]

                                                         ●

There's a typo in the book. The Parthenon was completed in 431 (four thirty-

                  ●

one) B.C., not 421 (four twenty-one) B.C.

Example 5:   Parallel phrases. In these constructions, there may be more than one
                    primary stress in each message unit.

                                      ●

This graph shows the *smoking habits of American females.

                ●   ●

In 1965 (nineteen sixty-five), | 34 (thirty-four) percent smoked;

                ●   ●

in 1975 (nineteen seventy-five), | 31 (thirty-one) percent smoked.

     ●   ●   ●   ●

An 85 (eighty-five) is a B; | a 75 (seventy-five) is a C.

Example 6:   Contradicting

                                  ●

A: Aren't you the TA for Stats 315 (three fifteen)?

                    ●   ●

B: I teach 316 (three sixteen). You must be thinking of Maria Gómez.

---

*compound noun

☛ **EXERCISE 9.**   Dialogs
a. Mark the stress on each compound number.
b. Mark the primary stress in each message unit.
c. Read each dialog aloud.

Situation 1. Two students studying in the dorm

A: It's so hot in here I can't even study! It must be seventy-five degrees!

B: Sorry to say, | it's eighty-five. I wonder what the *forecast is.

A: The radio said a high of ninety-two | and a low of seventy-two.

B: Maybe we should apply to the University of Alaska!

Situation 2. Two students working on a math problem

A: So if *x* equals 24 (twenty-four), | then *y* equals 34 (thirty-four).

B: But *y* equals 54 (fifty-four). What are we doing wrong?

Situation 3. A math student with a question

A: I'm confused. Is this *line segment supposed to be fifty-two inches | or fifty-six inches?

B: Neither. It's fifty-four inches.

Situation 4. In class

A: When you do the homework, | read all of the items first to find the easiest ones. For example, | I thought question 14 (fourteen) was easier than question 13 (thirteen).

B: Are you going to give us a chance for extra credit?

A: Yes. For extra credit you can try either question 22 (twenty-two) | or question 32 (thirty-two) | on page 79 (seventy-nine).

B: But those are on page 89 (eighty-nine), | not page 79 (seventy-nine).

A: OK, right. Sorry about that.

---

*compound noun

☛ **EXERCISE 10.**   Saying and Listening to Numbers with a Partner
a. Choose one of the items in each pair and read it aloud.
b. When you read an item, your partner will circle what he or she hears.
c. Check your partner's answer.
d. Take turns reading and circling.

14	40	15 times	50 times
15	50	17 weeks	70 weeks
16	60	18 pages	80 pages
17	70	19 days	90 days

☛ **EXERCISE 11.**   Explaining a Table
a. Study the table below.
b. Explain it to a partner, monitoring your stress on compound numbers.

Number of Babies Born in Two Regions

	Region A	Region B
1985	2,325	2,334
1990	2,395	2,026
1995	3,042	2,016
1996	3,287	1,997
1997	3,624	1,887

☞ **EXERCISE 12.**   General and Specific Academic Terms
   a. Choose two general or specific academic terms that could be used with numbers.
   b. Write two short dialogs or passages, each using at least one numerical expression.
   c. Mark the stress on each compound number and mark the primary stress in each message unit.
   d. Read each dialog or passage aloud several times.

Examples:

Chemistry

   A: What's the atomic number of cobalt?

               ●

   B: Twènty-seven.
   A: And what about argon?

              ●

   C: Èighteen.

Statistics

                                                       ○

     Suppose you conducted a survey of 874 (eight hundred seventy-four)

   ●   ●   ●

people. Four hundred twenty-seven were women, | and (447) four hundred

   ●   ●   ●

forty-seven were men. What is the ratio of men to women? What is the

          ●

percentage of each?

W-9E. Phrasal Verbs

☛ **EXERCISE 1.**   Listen to the following dialog and mark the primary stress with ● according to what you hear.

Situation: A is a TA, and B is a student who comes in during office hours.

A: Come in. Sit down.

B: I need to talk to you. I've spent two hours on problem 6, | but I can't figure it out!

A: Let's look at it. If there's a solution, | I'm sure we can come up with it.

Phrasal verbs consist of a main verb and one or two particles. Sometimes the main verb is stressed, and sometimes a particle is stressed. For phrasal verbs with one particle, there are two stress patterns. Phrasal verbs with two particles have one stress pattern.

Three Patterns for Phrasal Verbs		
Two Parts	**Two Parts**	**Three Parts**
Stress the Verb	Stress the Particle	Stress the First Particle
●	●	●
talk to	come in	come up with

Phrasal Verbs with Stress on the Verb (Type 1)

●	●	●	●
talk to	accuse of	warn about	ask for
●	●	●	●
look at	provide with	borrow from	rely on

When the particle is *about, against, at, for, from, of, on, to,* or *with,* the verb receives heavier stress.

> NOTE: When the verb refers to mental activity or communicating, the particle *on* does not receive stress. Otherwise, with other verbs, the particle *on* may be stressed.

☞ **EXERCISE 2.** Type 1 Phrasal Verbs
a. Mark the stress on the phrasal verbs with ●.
b. Read each dialog aloud.

Situation 1. Two TAs talking

A: What's wrong with this computer?

B: It's the one I warned you about.

A: Well, I need one I can rely on.

Situation 2. Two TAs talking

A: I was hoping Tom would be working with us.

B: I agree. I asked him to, | but I haven't heard from him.

Situation 3. Two TAs talking

A: What are you looking for?

B: My *lecture notes. I've looked everywhere I can think of.

A: What do you usually do with them | after you write them?

Phrasal Verbs with Stress on the Particle (Type 2)

●	●	●	●
come in	go away	bring up	take over

●	●	●	●
sit down	figure out	look into	put down

If a phrasal verb does **not** contain one of the nine particles found in type 1 phrasal verbs, heavier stress can go on the particle. These particles include *in, down, away, out, up, into, over, ahead, around, back, behind, by, off.*

☞ **EXERCISE 3.** Type 2 Phrasal Verbs
a. Mark the stress on the phrasal verbs with ●.
b. Read each passage aloud.

---

*compound noun

Situation 1. A TA in class

> Class, you'd better listen up. This next part is important, | so you'd better write it down.

Situation 2. A TA in class

> Your assignment for Friday takes a long time to work out, | so you need to plan ahead. I don't want you to get behind.

Situation 3. A TA in class

> I think some people are getting lost, | so let's go back. Look at the formula first. Check it over | and see if there's anything you left out.

Three-Part Phrasal Verbs

Three-part phrasal verbs always have heavier stress on the first particle.

●	●	●
get away with	look forward to	come up with
●	●	●
follow up on	get around to	show up for

☞ **EXERCISE 4.** Three-Part Phrasal Verbs
  a. Mark the stress on the phrasal verbs with ●.
  b. Read each passage aloud.

Situation 1. A TA in class

> Don't plagiarize. You can't get away with it.

Situation 2. A TA in a Spanish class

> If you're uncomfortable using the subjunctive, | maybe you need to brush up on it.

Situation 3. A TA in class

> If there's someone in your group you can't get along with, | come and talk to me.

Phrasal Verbs in Discourse

Of course, in discourse, phrasal verbs do not always receive primary stress (see Discourse Foundations D-5 in your core textbook for more information on primary stress). When the primary stress occurs elsewhere, type 1 phrasal verbs still have heavier stress on the verb than on the particle. By contrast, type 2 and type 3 phrasal verbs have equal stress on the verb and the particle after the verb.

Type 1 phrasal verbs

Heaviest stress on verb	Heavier stress on verb than particle
●	○ ●
I need to <u>talk to</u> you.	I need to <u>talk to</u> the professor.

Type 2 phrasal verbs

Heaviest stress on particle	Equal stress on verb and particle
●	○ ○ ●
We <u>left</u> it <u>out</u>.	We <u>left</u> it <u>out</u> deliberately.

Type 3 phrasal verbs

Heaviest stress on first particle	Equal stress on verb and first particle
●	○ ○ ●
You can't <u>get away with</u> it.	You can't <u>get away with</u> plagiarism.

> NOTE: There is a special stress pattern for type 2 phrasal verbs with noun objects. When a noun object precedes or follows the particle in type 2 phrasal verbs, it will receive the primary stress if it is the last content word in new information. The verb and particle have equal stress.
>
> | ○ ● ○ | ○ ○ ● |
> |---|---|
> | We <u>left</u> the graph <u>out</u>. | We <u>left out</u> the graph. |

☞ **EXERCISE 5.**   Phrasal Verbs in Discourse
                 a. Underline the phrasal verbs.
                 b. Mark the primary stress with ●.
                 c. Mark the stress on the unmarked phrasal verbs with ○.
                 d. Read each passage aloud.

Example: A TA in class

           ○   ●   ○   ○ ○   ●
           <u>Put</u> your pencils <u>down</u>. It's time to <u>pass in</u> your quizzes. Then you can

    ○   ○   ○ ●   ○   ●
    <u>go ahead</u> and <u>take off</u>. We'll <u>start with</u> Ohm's law next Monday.

Situation 1. A TA at the end of the semester

        When you hand your paper in, | I'll tell you when you can come by and

        pick it up.

Situation 2. Office hours

    A: I don't think you're getting at the problem | if you don't consider inflation.

    B: I guess I've been dealing with this in completely the wrong way.

    A: Think about it. What happens when inflation goes up?

Situation 3. TA in lab

        When you're finished with your *lab report, | don't forget to clean up

        your space.

Situation 4. A TA in lab

        Before you leave the lab, | don't forget to clean up.

_____

*compound noun

Situation 5. A TA in class

I'm going to put your next assignment off until next week. You need to figure out how to use the scanner, | and we won't have time to set it up until Monday.

Situation 6. A TA in class

If you've caught up on everything in chapter 6, | just move ahead to chapter 7.

Situation 7. Two TAs talking

Look at this. Two more students cheated on this assignment. We shouldn't put up with this.

☞ **EXERCISE 6.**   a. Mark the primary stress with ●.
b. Mark the stress on the unmarked phrasal verbs with ○.
c. Read each phrasal verb aloud.
d. Take turns asking and answering the questions with a partner. Give reasons or details to support your answers.

1. If a magician would grant you three wishes, | what would you ask for?

2. What kind of music do you usually listen to?

3. If you could move away, | where would you go?

4. What kind of person is it difficult for you to put up with?

5. When you are sad or depressed, | what helps you cheer up?

6. Who is someone you can always depend on?

7. If you could plan a perfect dinner, | what would it consist of?

8. At night, do you prefer to stay in | or go out?

9. When you're with your best friend, | what do you most like to talk about?

10. When you think about the future, | what do you look forward to?

☞ **EXERCISE 7.**   a. Write two dialogs or short passages. Each one should have
  • at least one general academic term or one specific academic term and
  • at least one phrasal verb.
  b. Mark the primary stress on message units containing phrasal verbs.
  c. Mark the stress on the unmarked phrasal verbs with ○.
  d. Read each dialog or passage aloud.

Examples:

Biology

                ○   ●
A: We have already talked about the epidermis. Underneath the epidermis is a

                              ●
layer of skin called the dermis. Does anyone remember what it consists of?

B: It's mostly connective tissue.

                             ○   ●
A: Right. It also contains blood vessels, and sweat glands pass through it.

Greek mythology

      Clytie was the daughter of Oceanus and Tethys. She and Apollo were in

        ○   ●
love, but Apollo broke it off. According to the myth, she was so heart-

        ○   ○   ●
broken that she turned into a sunflower.

APPENDIXES

The following resources supplement the material in *Speechcraft: Workbook for International TA Discourse.*

The oral practice projects can be adapted according to students' needs by adjusting the time constraints, the focus of the content, and the focus of the pronunciation topics. When such adjustments are made, the oral practice projects can also be repeated throughout the course.

Similarly, the Checklist for Covert Rehearsal is intended to be used repeatedly throughout the course and beyond.

APPENDIX 1:
ORAL PRACTICE PROJECTS

PROJECT 1: THREE-MINUTE TALK

Phase 1: Preparing Your Talk

1. Prepare your talk as if you were speaking to novices in your field of study. Choose a topic that is basic enough for your classmates to understand.
2. Use at least three specific academic terms and three general academic terms from your lists.
3. Prepare the text of your talk. You may write it out word for word or use a well-developed outline with key phrases and transitions included.
4. Rewrite your text based on the revisions your instructor suggests. Divide the key phrases of your talk into appropriate message units and mark the primary stress.
5. Rehearse your talk at least three times. Use the Checklist for Covert Rehearsal (App. 2) to concentrate on the features of pronunciation that are relevant for you.

Phase 2: Recording Your Talk
Make a tape recording of your talk and hand it in.

Phase 3: Conference with Your Instructor
Your instructor will help you to focus on areas in which you need to improve.

Phase 4: In-Class Presentation

1. Rehearse your talk. Use the Checklist for Covert Rehearsal and the feedback your instructor has given you.
2. Give your three-minute talk to your classmates. Your talk will be videotaped.

Phase 5: Self-Evaluation

1. With your instructor, select four topics from the Checklist for Covert Rehearsal to focus on.
2. Watch the videotape and write down up to four instances of each topic you
   selected. Analyze your performance by marking in corrections where you
   need to and putting a check mark (✓) by the selected words or phrases
   you produced correctly.

Phase 6: In-Class Presentation
Rehearse your talk three more times and present it again to your classmates.

PROJECT 2: FIVE-MINUTE TALK WITH QUESTIONS

Phase 1: Preparing Your Talk

1. Prepare your talk as if you were speaking to novices in your field of study. Choose a topic that is basic enough for your classmates to understand.
2. Use at least three specific academic terms and three general academic terms from your lists.
3. In addition, plan **two questions** about your topic to ask your classmates. Select two different question types you have studied, e.g., choice question, *yes/no* question, narrowed question.
4. Prepare the text of your talk. You may write it out word for word or use a well-developed outline with key phrases and transitions included.

   a. Write out word for word the two questions you have prepared.
   b. Identify the type of question each is, e.g., choice question, *yes/no* question, narrowed question, etc.
   c. Mark the primary stress on each question and write down what kind of intonation it should have.

5. Rewrite your text based on the revisions your instructor suggests. Divide your talk into appropriate message units and mark the primary stress.
6. Rehearse your talk at least three times. Use the Checklist for Covert Rehearsal (App. 2) to concentrate on the stress and intonation of the questions and other features of pronunciation that are relevant for you.

Phase 2: Recording Your Talk
Make a tape recording of your talk and hand it in.

Phase 3: Conference with Your Instructor
Your instructor will help you to focus on areas in which you need to improve.

Phase 4: In-Class Presentations

1. Rehearse your talk. Use the Checklist for Covert Rehearsal and the feedback your instructor has given you.
2. Give your five-minute talk to your classmates, asking the questions you prepared.
3. Practice your talk using feedback you receive in class.
4. Present the talk again to your classmates.

PROJECT 3: INTERVIEWING A TA

In this assignment, you will interview a native English-speaking TA from your department and describe him or her to the rest of the class.

Phase 1: Preparing and Doing the Interview

1. Set up the interview. Identify a TA in your department who is a native speaker of English. Explain the assignment and ask him or her to spend five to ten minutes talking with you. Make sure that the TA is aware that the interview will be tape-recorded.
2. Determine the questions you will ask. Bring to class five questions that you plan to ask the TA. In class, you will practice the pronunciation of these questions, discuss possible responses you might get from the TA, and plan follow-up questions.
3. Do the interview. Tape-record it! Talk to the TA for at least five minutes using the questions you have prepared. Be sure to use good question stress and intonation.

Phase 2: Transcription
Choose a two-minute segment of the tape. Write down the exact words that you hear—your voice and the TA's.

Phase 3: Analysis
On your transcription of the entire two-minute segment, mark

- message units (|)
- primary stress (●)
- compound nouns.

Hand in your transcription.

Phase 4: In-Class Summary

1. Summarize your interview. Plan a coherent two- to three-minute talk in which you

   - "introduce" the TA you interviewed,
   - describe him or her based on what you learned from your questions, and
   - give a brief conclusion about the TA and the interview.

2. Rehearse your talk at least three times using the Checklist for Covert Rehearsal (App. 2).
3. Present your talk to the class.

Appendix 2: Checklist for Covert Rehearsal

This checklist can be used any time you do covert rehearsal (see Groundwork G-1 for a definition of covert rehearsal). It is particularly valuable for preparing oral presentations.

Before your next oral presentation, select some of the following topic areas to focus on. Use a separate sheet of paper to write down specific examples of each topic you select. When you practice, focus specifically on the topics you have chosen. Try to monitor yourself as carefully as possible and make corrections as you see fit.

After your oral presentation, reconsider the topics you selected to work on.

- If you feel you made progress on that topic, put a plus (+) on the line.
- If you feel you did not do as well as you expected, put a minus (-) on the line.
- If you are not sure how you did, put a question mark (?) on the line.
- Give examples from your talk.

Focus

_____ Vowel and Consonant Sounds (Specify: _____)

_____ Message Units

My message units should be ___ shorter / ___ longer / ___ more meaningful.

_____	Intonation	_____	Alternations
_____	Linking	_____	Trimming

_____ Primary Stress (Specify domains: _____)

_____	Word Stress	_____	-*s* ending
_____	Compound Nouns	_____	-*ed* ending

_____ Pacing. Check one: I would like to talk ___ slower / ___ faster.

_____ Volume. Check one: I would like to talk ___ louder / ___ softer.

_____ Other: _____

_____

APPENDIX 3: ANSWERS TO ITEMS

DISCOURSE DOMAINS

D-8. Comparing and Contrasting

Exercise 1

●: teaching, positive, negative, students, alike, not, understand, example, abstract, concrete, liberal, conservative, sciences, languages, rhetoric, physics, some, socializing, studying, others, yourself, energetic, relaxed, high, low, way, happen, unfortunately, favor, identify, dis- (of disfavor), misunderstand, easiest, rewarding, differences, equally

Exercise 2

Dia. 1 ●: Quixote; Yes, English, Spanish

Dia. 2 ●: tell, 1, 2; experiment

Pass. 1 ●: religions, poly- (of polytheistic), mono- (of monotheistic)

Pass. 2 ●: expected, audit, drop

Exercise 4

Dia. 1 ●: party; Well, your, mine

Dia. 2 ●: English; pronunciation; OK, one, only

Pass. 1 ●: C, admit, A, B

Pass. 2 ●: again, nucleus, eu- (of eukaryote), pro- (of prokaryote)

Exercise 6

Dia. 1 ●: I; didn't, Russia

Dia. 2 ●: recital; course, performing, soloist

Dia. 3 ●: assistantship; did, late, taken

Exercise 8

Pass. 1 ●: numerator, top, denominator, bottom

Pass. 2 ●: first, describe, second, use

Pass. 3 ●: references, alphabetical, figures, numerical

Pass. 4 ●: Justin, in- (of inductive), Bill, de- (of deductive)

Exercise 10 ●:

1. Graduate, under- (of undergraduate)
2. Professors, teaching
3. American, Japanese
4. Cooperation, competition
5. Big, small
6. Lecturing, discussions
7. Speaking, writing

8. English, Chinese
9. party, concert
10. Going, hosting

D-9. Lists and Series

Exercise 1

●: 115 |, class |, Mondays |, Wednesdays |, Fridays |, poetry |, reading |, analyzing |, writing |, day |, grade |, supplies |, notebook |, tape |, disk |, computer |, textbook |, Poetry |, Bookstore |, Follett's |, library |, exams |, papers |, final |, project |, lot |, manageable |, far

Exercise 2 ●:

1. started |, computer |, diskette |, application
2. numbers |, mean |, variance|, deviation
3. young |, innocent |, love
4. Brazil |, Ecuador |, Peru |, Chile |, capital |, population |, monetary (unit)|, exports
5. are |, do |, can |, English
6. lab |, campus |, community
7. test |, pencil |, paper (over) |, hand
8. discussion (section) |, lecture |, A.M.
9. gram (stain)|, slowly |, carefully |, steadily
10. presentation |, first |, second |, third |, fourth

Exercise 3 ●:

1. Eat |, drink |, merry
2. came |, saw |, conquered
3. bed |, rise |, healthy |, wealthy |, wise
4. fade |, crumble |, fall |, endure
5. forget |, remember |, understand
6. education |, means |, morality |, sobriety |, enterprise |, industry |, present
7. minds |, language |, science |, religion |, opinions |, fancies
8. words |, friendship |, thoughts |, desires |, expectations |, shared |, unacclaimed

Exercise 4 ● (Words in parentheses do not receive primary stress.)

1. frequently |, before (the experiment) |, during (the experiment) |, after (the experiment)
2. photosynthesis |, how (it happens) |, why (it happens) |, when (it happens)
3. Aesthetic (factors) |, structural (factors) |, economic (factors) |, architecture
4. Enthusiastic (teachers) |, organized (teachers) |, knowledgeable (teachers) |, ratings
5. collect (the sample) |, identify (the sample) |, analyze (the sample)

D-10. Choice Questions and Answers

Exercise 1

●: wrong, worried, sick, tired; worried, students, whispering, class; well, poorly; well, disturbing, think, deal, ignore; deal, rest, too; OK, right, during, after; after, pressure

Exercise 2 (Words in parentheses do not receive primary stress.)

Sit. 1 ●:   came, see, nine (o'clock class) |, eleven (o'clock class); eleven, window; yeah, thought, first (assignment) |, second (assignment); second, easy

Sit. 2 ●:   names, your (handwriting) |, his; mine, his

Sit. 3 ●:   assignment, Before (the quiz) |, after (the quiz); After, relaxed

Sit. 4 ●:   nine; fifty (nine) |, sixty (nine); Oh, Fifty, books

Sit. 5 ●:   agree (with the theory) |, dis(agree with it); dis(agrees); OK, strongly (disagrees) |, mildly (disagrees); mildly, part

Sit. 6 ●:   Friday |, Monday; me, depends, essay |, answer |, choice |, what; choice; Friday; rest, Friday |, Monday |, other (day); Friday

D-11. Yes/No *Questions and Answers*

Exercise 1

●:   test; Yes, hour; Yes, bell, else; credit; might, professor, know, way, chromosomes; Why, on; not, final

Exercise 2

Sit. 1 ●:   microscope; broken; sure

Sit. 2 ●:   Kant; really

Sit. 3 ●:   word, try; know, complicated

Sit. 4 ●:   exam, give; OK, first

Sit. 5 ●:   adviser; talk; mind, help

Sit. 6 ●:   star; No, light; sun; Yes

Sit. 7 ●:   valid; Yes, shows; reliable; sure, investigated

Sit. 8 ●:   TA; Yes, 110; good; bad

Sit. 9 ●:   term; plagiarized; agree, intentionally; possible

Exercise 3

Sit. 1 ●:   curve, test, normal; No; why, Should; necessarily, homogeneous

Sit. 2 ●:   laser, on; know, check

Sit. 3 ●:   Curtis, in; saw, find

Sit. 4 ●:   Teachers; on; Yes, Congratulations

Sit. 5 ●:   stacks; with, lost; Yes, Morgan's

Exercise 4

Sit. 1 ●:   2:00, be; Yes, want, long, you

Sit. 2 ●:   Friday, substitute, suggestions; Collins, know; No; George, him; Yeah, idea

Exercise 5

Sit. 1 ●:   Japanese; do

Sit. 2 ●:   paper; haven't

Sit. 3 ●:   presentation; am; quiz; not

Sit. 4 ●:   number; is; six; isn't

Sit. 5 ●:   experiment, variable; not, in- (of independent)

Sit. 6 ●:   staff; should, wasn't

Sit. 7 ●:   students; might, familiar

Exercise 7

●:   far; with; sense; following; good; ask

D-12. Tag Questions and Answers

Exercise 1

●: homework, trouble, haven't; have, class, am; not, help; Maybe, 4:00, isn't; Yes, free, are; lab, dropped, fine; OK, Oh, time, won't, 4:30; Sure, lot

Melody: L, H, L, H, H

Exercise 2

Sit. 1 ●: quiz, didn't (L); did, up, can't (H); think, class

Sit. 2 ●: class, isn't (L); is, coming, aren't (H); know, swamped

Sit. 3 ●: Beth, poem; sure, Whitman, was (H); was

Sit. 4 ●: written, is (L); really, cite, are (H); am, criticize

Sit. 5 ●: prelims, passed, didn't (L); Yes, relief, isn't (L); Definitely

Sit. 6 ●: handout; copied, have (H); Why, correction, do (H); late

D-13. Information Questions and Answers

Exercise 1

●: started, homework, one, Ben, answer; 89; OK, different; I; you; 85; be, completely; Really, was; 374, right; I, together

Exercise 2

Sit. 1 ●: method; problem; Right, second; topic

Sit. 2 ●: sulfur; meteorites; Yes, characteristics; solid

Sit. 3 ●: force; momentum; OK, calculate; acceleration

Sit. 4 ●: axis; test; vertical; number

Exercise 3

Sit. 1 ●: probe, see; for; spectroscopy

Sit. 2 ●: quiz, be; Friday

Sit. 3 ●: drug; blood; OK, after; change

Sit. 4 ●: office, quiz; OK, is; Lab, floor

Sit. 5 ●: microscope, think; know, is; cancer

Sit. 6 ●: computer; Yes, lost; were; desk

Exercise 4

Sit. 1 ●: Ages, write; Comedy; Right, another, he; Canterbury

Sit. 2 ●: tree; maple; Good, another, this; red

Exercise 5

Sit. 1 ●: recognize; seven

Sit. 2 ●: graph, women; Clerical; Right, lowest; Mechanical

Sit. 3 ●: sales; percent; B; 40, advertising

Sit. 4 ●: book; Oh, yours, mistake

Sit. 5 ●: mail; for; you

Sit. 6 ●: lab; I'll, turn

D-14. Narrowed Questions and Answers

Exercise 1

●: Manifesto; Marx; Right, When; 1800s; Yes, When; middle, 1848; Exactly, Why; conditions; Right, later, else; Kapital

Exercise 2

Sit. 1 ●: research; validity; OK, type; Internal; Good, kind; test

Sit. 2 ●: assignment; Which; 96; OK, kinds; trapezoid

Sit. 3 ●: library; yeah, Which; public; Great, anyway, Where; level, back

Sit. 4 ●: paper; March; When; syllabus, week; no, physics, When; fourth, Tuesday

Exercise 3

Sit. 1 ●: study, subjects (Info Q); increased; second (Info Q); same; Why (Narrowed Q); stimulus

Sit. 2 ●: conclusion (Info Q); I; else (Narrowed Q); I, too; dis- (of disagrees) (Info Q); I; Why (Narrowed Q); support

D-15. Repetition Questions and Answers

Exercise 1

●: hall, review, Tuesday; When's; Tuesday, louder, Cortés, what; Incas; Incas; No, wait, Aztecs; Right, Aztecs, Mexico, year; 1519; hear, 1519; Yeah; Excellent, 1519

Exercise 2

Sit. 1 ●: 12; pounds; Forty (RQ); think, fifty; Right, Fifty, get

Sit. 2 ●: book, regression; page; 45; Which (RQ); 45, 2

Sit. 3 ●: review, programming, what (RQ); while; right, 7; Do; do (RQ); Yes

Sit. 4 ●: final, join; Maybe, cover; book; make, down, when (RQ); Tonight, 7:30; where (RQ); Ben's, lives; Ben (RQ), Yeah, ride, Who (RQ); Jeff; Great, call, Thanks

WORD STRESS DOMAINS

W-5A. Final Key Rule Endings -ion, -iate, -ial, *etc.*

Exercise 1

1. cónsciously
2. quéstions, evaluátion
3. equátions, conclúsions
4. permíssion, quéstions, apprópriately
5. inítiating, discússion
6. corréction
7. informátion, examinátions

Exercise 2

1. introdúction
2. esséntial, informátion
3. diréctions
4. cónscious
5. revísions, explanátions
6. crúcial, instrúctions, precaútions
7. ánxious, région
8. congratulátions

Exercise 3

Caprícious, Definítion, critéria, inítially, allegátions, esséntial, Caprícious, reáction, informátion, Administrátion

W5-B. Nonfinal Key Rule Endings -ional, iary, *etc.*

Exercise 1

1. inítiative
2. revolútionary
3. perféctionist
4. collóquialisms
5. unméntionable
6. instrúctional
7. appréciative
8. dispropórtionate
9. tradítional, unconvéntional
10. concíliatory, retáliatory
11. overspécialize
12. plágiarism
13. practítioner, theoretícian
14. rátionalize
15. benefíciary
16. conversátionalist

W-6A. V/VC Rule Endings -al, -ous, ic

Exercise 1

Sit. 1. theorétical; anónymous, práctical; experiméntal
Sit. 2. infórmal, génerous; rígorous; specífically, crítical
Sit. 3. económics; monótonous, archáic; ridículous
Sit. 4. éthics; oríginal, númerous, strúctural; circúitous

Exercise 2

Reading 1. Nonvérbal, treméndous, óral, nonvérbal, cúltural, contínuous, márvelous, géneral, conspícuous, Overzeálous, total, nonvérbal, týpical, periódically, infórmal, cásual, pérsonal, enórmous, nonvérbal
Reading 2. governméntal, treméndously, phýsical, génerous, crítical, governméntal, génerally, grádually, ideológical, indivídual, prósperous, technológical, artístic

Exercise 3

1. contínually
2. unúsual
3. Númerous
4. vígorously
5. contínuously
6. séxually

W-6B. V/VC Rule Endings -V*nt,* -V*nce,* -V*ncy*
Exercise 1
  1. intélligent
  2. fréquently, acquaíntances
  3. cónfidence
  4. indepéndent
  5. linguístic, rélevant
  6. perfórmance
  7. dóminant
  8. ígnorance, nátural
  9. cúlturally, dífferences
  10. ínference, contéxtual, linguístic
  11. dóminant
  12. redúndancy, accéptance
Exercise 3
  1. árgument
  2. signíficant
  3. intélligence
  4. impórtance, pérmanently

W-7A. Left Rule Endings -y/-i *on Long Words*
Exercise 1
  Reading 1. idéntified, reálity, Personálity, Psychólogy, humánities, chémistry, quánti-
       fied, humánities, Biólogy, terminólogy, humánities, regulárity, creatívity
  Reading 2. fratérnities, sorórities, fratérnities, sorórities, idéntified, fratérnity, com-
       múnity, socíeties, (céremonies is an exception), clássify, individuálity,
       opportúnity, actívities, philánthropy, commúnity, sorórities, fratérnities,
       quálity
Exercise 2
  secúrity, sátisfying, opportúnity, stabílity, sátisfying, anxíety, authórity, abílity,
  clárity, opportúnity, creatívity, philósophy

W-7B. Left Rule Endings -ate, -acy
Exercise 1
  1. commúnicate, cóncentrate, áccuracy
  2. coórdinator, idéntify, quálified, cándidate, líteracy
  3. dévastated, quálity
  4. cálculate, tábulate, córrelate
  5. methodólogy, símplify, unfórtunately, appróximate, reálity
  6. éfficacy, pólicy
  7. clárify, íntricacies
  Sit. 1. éducated; Univérsity; gráduate; kinesiólogy
  Sit. 2. inádequacies; ináccurate
  Sit. 3. córporate, pólicy; ánnotated, bibliógraphy, productívity

Reading. univérsities, íntegrate, quálity, undergráduate, priórity, univérsity, technól-ogy, divérsity, éducating, undergráduates, cómplicated, univérsity, ad-mínistrators, coórdinate, socíety, quálity, céntury, ádequacy

Exercise 2

commúnicate, éducate, intímidate, artículate, démonstrate, coórdinate, cóncentrate, írritate, exággerate, íntegrate, facílitate, accómmodate, oríginate, hésitate, colláb-orate, mótivate

W-8A. Prefixes and Stress

Exercise 1

1. provócative, pro-; expósitory
2. ~~retro~~spéctive; ~~contra~~díctory
3. impréssive, im-; ~~extra~~sénsory
4. cémetery; inconclúsive, con-
5. impercéptive, per; accúsatory, ac-
6. ~~inter~~áctive; coóperative
7. affírmative, af-; nondiscríminatory
8. incísive, in-; ~~counter~~intúitive
9. advísory, ad-; obsérvatory, ob-
10. législative; appéllative, ap-
11. occlúsive, oc-; cápillaries; córonary, ártery
12. succéssive, suc-; corréctive, cor-
13. comprehénsive, pre-; cógnitive
14. ~~over~~aggréssive, ag-; efféctive, ef-
15. ~~intro~~spéctive; ~~super~~sénsitive
16. oppréssive, op; abrásive, ab-
17. subcóntrary, sub-; refútatory, re-
18. prodúctive, pro-; commúnicative

Exercise 2

1. introspéctive, none
2. efféctive, ef-
3. cátegories, none
4. intúitive, none
5. cógnitive, none
6. apprehénsive, pre-
7. téntative, none
8. afféctive, af-
9. subjéctive, sub-
10. imáginative, none
11. percéptive, per-
12. atténtive, at-
13. expénditure, none
14. assértive, as-
15. inténsive, in-
16. spéculative, none

Review

assímilative, profánatory, músculature, appéllative, reféctory, ~~super~~aggréssive, compárative, admínistrative, predíctive, cáricature, sécondary, córonary, ~~counter~~prodúctive, compúlsory, distíllery, recríminatory, repétitive, cháncellery, itínerary, contémporary

1. super-, counter-. Neutral prefixes should be ignored.
2. No part: assímilature, músculature, admínistrative, cáricature, sécondary, córonary, recríminatory, repétitive, cháncellery, itínerary, contémporary
   Whole: appéllative, superaggréssive
   Part: profánatory, reféctory, compárative, predíctive, ~~counter~~prodúctive, compúlsory, distíllery
3. the vowel letter
4. when it does not begin a word or does not follow a neutral prefix: admínistrative, itínerary

W-8B. Prefix Rule Endings -ary, -ery, -ory, -ive

Exercise 1

Sit. 1. Hístory, Sécondary, Perspéctives; Eleméntary, supervísory
Sit. 2. vóluntarily or voluntárily; extraórdinary; Extraórdinarily or Extraordinárily, extémporary; discóveries, árteries, córonary; dórmitories
Sit. 3. documéntary, Húngary, objéctive; mílitary, cómmentary
Sit. 4. impréssive, compúlsory; advísory

Exercise 2

Adjectives

1. compúlsory
2. extémporary
3. distínctive
4. sánitary
5. cógnitive
6. mómentary
7. contradíctory
8. imáginary

Nouns

1. dórmitory
2. fúgitive
3. itínerary
4. refínery
5. obítuary
6. objéctive
7. cátegory
8. mónastery

Exercise 3

Hístory, Hístory, Discóveries, introdúctory, Cógnitive, Interáctive, compúlsory, líbrary, Perspéctives, suppleméntary, sécretary

W-8C. Prefix Rule Endings -ative, -atory, -ature

Exercise 1

1. explóratory, provócative
2. authóritative, líterature
3. spéculative, éducative
4. invéstigative, quálitative, quántitative
5. explánatory, represéntative
6. consérvative, recapítulative
7. sígnature, commémorative

Exercise 2

Perspéctives, Admínistrative, Compárative, Commúnicative, Contémporary, Líterature, Quántitative, Perspéctives, Júdicature, Labóratory or Láboratory, Consérvatory, Líbrary, Líterature, Obsérvatory

W-9A. Compound Nouns 1

Exercise 1

1. biology
2. axis
3. literature
4. assignments
5. variable
6. sample
7. grades
8. grammar

Exercise 3

In all situations, the first word of the compound noun receives ○.

Sit. 1. lab assistant; SPEAK test; proficiency test, tape recorder; practice test, Listening Lab

Sit. 2. computer lab; identification card

Sit. 3. graduate program; course work, department head, research assistant

Sit. 4. computer program, test scores; record keeping; data analysis, discussion sections

Sit. 5. history class, lecture notes; review session; essay test, Iron Age; weekend

Sit. 6. bookstore, computer paper, textbook, rhetoric class; lab report, notebook

Exercise 4

In all compound nouns, the first word receives ○.

Exercise 7

1. mouse pad
2. keyboard
3. screen saver
4. desktop
5. operating system
6. password

W-9B. Compound Nouns 2

Exercise 1

   ○: Hart, Gonzales, Goldstein

Exercise 7

   ○: E, L, A, bag, ring, soup, seminar, vacation, class

W-9D. Compound Numbers

Exercise 1

   ○: The last number in each compound

Exercise 2

   ○: The last number in each compound

Exercise 3

   Sit. 1. ○: -teen

         ●: -two

   Sit. 2. ○: -teen (of 19), -seven;

         ●: -five; -one, -teen (of 116)

   Sit. 3. ○: -teenth (of 17th); five (of 45)

         ●: -first (of 21st)

Exercise 4

○	＼	○
four-	teen	cents
thir-	teen	chapters
nine-	teen	grams
forty-	six	students
seventy-	five	types
ninety-	four	years
fifty-	three	acres
ninety-	nine	days
fifty-	six	pounds

Exercise 5

   Sit. 1. ●: class; Sure, -five, talk; ditches; Fine, long

         ○: fif-; thirty-, six-

   Sit. 2. ●: test, correct; -teen

         ○: seventy-

   Sit. 3. ●: control; subjects; experimental; -two

         ○: twenty-

   Sit. 4. ●: miles, rate; hour; Right, -two; seven

         ○: six-, twenty-; four-

Exercise 6

a.

`	○
twenty-	five
thirty-	six
thir-	teen
sixty-	five
twenty-	four
four-	teen
fifty-	two
thirty-	one
six-	teen
twenty-	six

d.

○	`	○
twenty-	five	cents
thirty-	six	inches
thir-	teen	heart
sixty-	five	days
twenty-	four	hours
four-	teen	carats
fifty-	two	weeks
thirty-	one	days
six-	teen	ounces
twenty-	six	letters

e. ●: year, alphabet, playing, pound, yard, quarter, gold, day, January, year

Exercise 8

eighty-, seventy-; twenty-, thirty-

Exercise 9

Sit. 1. ●: study, degrees; say, eighty-, forecast; high, ninety-, low, seventy- (of 72); Alaska

○: seventy- (of 75)

Sit. 2. ●: *x*, twenty-, *y,* thirty-; fifty-, wrong

Sit. 3. ●: confused, -two, -six; Neither, -four

Sit. 4. ●: homework, easiest, example, four-, thir-; credit; Yes, twenty-, thirty-, -nine; eighty-, seventy-; right, Sorry

W-9E. Phrasal Verbs

Exercise 1

●: in, down; talk, 6, out; look, solution, up

Exercise 2

Sit. 1. ●: warned; rely

Sit. 2. ●: working; asked, heard

Sit. 3. ●: looking; think; do

Exercise 3

Sit. 1. ●: up, down

Sit. 2. ●: out, ahead, behind

Sit. 3. ●: back, over, out

Exercise 4
   Sit. 1. ●: away
   Sit. 2. ●: up
   Sit. 3. ●: along, talk
Exercise 5
   Sit. 1. <u>hand in,</u> <u>come by,</u> <u>pick up</u>
      ●: paper, up
      ○: hand, in, come, by, pick
   Sit. 2. <u>getting at</u>; <u>dealing with</u>; <u>Think about,</u> <u>goes up</u>
      ●: problem, inflation; way; Think, up
      ○: getting; dealing; goes
   Sit. 3. <u>finished with,</u> <u>clean up</u>
      ●: lab, space
      ○: finished, clean, up
   Sit. 4. <u>clean up</u>
      ●: lab, up
      ○: clean
   Sit. 5. <u>put off,</u> <u>figure out,</u> <u>set up</u>
      ●: week, scanner, Monday
      ○: put, off, figure, out, set, up
   Sit. 6. <u>caught up on,</u> <u>move ahead to</u>
      ●: 6, 7
      ○: caught, up, move, ahead
   Sit. 7. <u>Look at,</u> <u>cheated on,</u> <u>put up with</u>
      ●: Look, assignment, up
      ○: cheated, put, up
Exercise 6
   1. ●: wishes, ask
   2. ●: listen
   3. ●: away, go
      ○: move
   4. ●: up
      ○: put
   5. ●: depressed, up
      ○: cheer
   6. ●: depend
   7. ●: dinner, consist
   8. ●: in, out
      ○: stay, go
   9. ●: friend, talk
   10. ●: future, forward
      ○: think, look